THE MARS PROJECT

THE MARS PROJECT

JOURNEYS BEYOND THE COLD WAR

SPARK M. MATSUNAGA

HILL AND WANG

NEW YORK

A division of Farrar, Straus and Giroux

Library of Congress Cataloging-in-Publication Data
Matsunaga, Spark M.
The Mars project.
Bibliography: p.
1. Space flight to Mars—International coopera-
tion.   I. Title.
TL799.M3M38   1986   387.8   86-350

To the memory of my father
Kingoro Matsunaga

ACKNOWLEDGMENTS

I have had the privilege of serving as a member of the United States Congress since 1963. To acknowledge fully all that I have gained in learning and fellowship from my colleagues in the House of Representatives and the Senate is an impossible task. I hope this book will contribute to the ongoing and open congressional dialogue concerning United States policy in the Space Age.

During four years of active involvement with the space cooperation issue, I consulted dozens of space scientists, either in person or through correspondence. Among those to whom I am indebted are Dr. Arden L. Albee, Dr. Lew Allen, Dr. Bernard F. Burke, Dr. Thomas M. Donahue, Dr. Tom Gehrels, Dr. Don Hall, Dr. James W. Head, Dr. John Jefferies, Dr. Charles Kennell, Dr. S. M. Krimigis, Dr. Eugene H. Levy, Dr. Harold Masursky, Dr. Thomas B. McCord, Dr. David Morrison, Dr. Tobias Owen, Dr. I. V. Rosool, Dr. John A. Simpson, Dr. Bradford A. Smith, Dr. Verner Soumi, Dr. James E. Tillman, Dr. Charles Townes, Dr. Gerald J. Wasserburg.

The officers of the Planetary Society, including President Carl

Sagan, Vice-President Bruce Murray, and Executive Director Louis Friedman, were a continuing source of information, inspiration, and support, and I hope their most worthy enterprise continues to flourish and reach the ever-widening audience it deserves.

Other members of the rapidly growing community of space specialists whom I wish to thank are Vance Brand, Leonard David, Dr. Ben Finney, James Harford, Christopher C. Kraft, Jr., Valery Kubasov, Alexei Leonov, Dr. John Logsdon, Dr. John L. McLucas, James Michener, James E. Oberg, Dr. Thomas O. Paine, Charles R. Pellegrino, Lee Saegesser, Donald K. Slayton, Marcia Smith, Thomas P. Stafford, Mark Washburn, Robert Weil.

To Isaac Asimov and Arthur C. Clarke, I convey my special thanks for their personal contributions, which in both cases required interrupting heavy schedules on short notice. David Morrison and Carl Sagan showed the same generosity in reviewing the manuscript for technical errors and calling them to my attention with utmost grace.

Indeed, although its subject matter had been percolating for some time, this entire book was written under considerable pressure, on weekends and at every other spare moment during seven months of busy congressional activity. In meeting that tense schedule, I found Arthur Wang's editorial assistance indispensable, including his persistent encouragement when the going was toughest. I am also deeply grateful to Russell Galen for having faith in *The Mars Project* when it was only a germinating idea, and for making sure it found its way into print in good hands.

The title came from a treatise by Wernher von Braun, first published in West Germany in 1952 as a magazine article entitled "Das Marsprojekt," then reissued in the United States in 1953 as a book: *The Mars Project*. It is a highly technical document, but, as with all von Braun's work, it is illuminated by a bold vision of humanity's future in space. Herman Melville wrote: "Give me a condor's quill! Give me Vesuvius' crater for an inkstand!" So it was with von Braun, and I am one of the many to benefit from his contributions.

ACKNOWLEDGMENTS

Finally, to Harvey Meyerson, a devoted friend and adviser, my heartfelt gratitude. Had it not been for his thought-provoking suggestions, encouragement, and assistance during weekends and holidays, and over many a cup of tea, this book would not have been written in the short time that it was.

For the final product, its observations and conclusions, I take full responsibility.

S.M.M.

Washington, D.C.
November 1985

CONTENTS

TWO

OPENING THE PATH

THREE

UNEXPECTED POSSIBILITIES

FOUR

THE MOUNTAIN MOVES

FIVE

A SPACE POLICY FOR
THE SPACE AGE

APPENDIXES

BIBLIOGRAPHY   213

FOREWORD

THE SNOWS OF OLYMPUS

In 1972, for only the third time in history, mankind discovered a new world.

It happened first in 1492. The impact of that discovery was immediate, its ultimate benefits incalculable. It created a new civilization, and revivified an old one.

The second date, not quite so famous, is 1610. In the spring of that year, Galileo turned his primitive "optic tube" toward the Moon, and saw with his own eyes that Earth is not unique. Floating out there a quarter of a million miles away was another world of mountains and valleys and great shining plains—empty, virginal—awaiting, like Michelangelo's Adam, the touch of life. And on 20 July 1969 life came, riding on a pillar of fire.

The third new world was not found by sailing ship or telescope; yet, like the two earlier discoveries, it was a shocking surprise that resulted in the overthrow of long-cherished beliefs. No one knew that such a place existed, and when the evidence started to accumulate, many scientists were literally unable to believe their eyes.

This new world was almost twice the diameter of the Moon,

with land area four times as large as both Americas. And it had the most spectacular scenery ever discovered.

Think of the Grand Canyon, the greatest natural wonder of the United States. Then quadruple its depth and multiply its width five times, to an incredible seventy-five miles. Finally—imagine it spanning the whole continent, from Los Angeles to New York. Such is the scale of the canyon that is carved across the face of *this* new world.

Nor is that the planet's most awesome feature, for it is dominated by volcanoes dwarfing any on Earth. The mightiest, Nix Olympica—the Snows of Olympus—is almost three times the height of Everest, and more than three hundred miles across. Those volcanoes are slumbering now, but not long ago—as the Universe measures time—they were blasting into the thin atmosphere all the chemicals of life, including water; there are dried-up riverbeds that give clear indication of recent flash floods—the first evidence ever found for running water outside our Earth.

By now, you may have guessed the identity of this new world. It is Mars—the *real* Mars, not the imaginary one in which we believed until the Mariner and Viking space probes swept away the illusions of decades. It will be years before we absorb all their lessons; but already it seems that Mars, not the Moon, will be our main order of business in the century to come.

This news may be received with less than enthusiasm when nonmilitary space budgets are being cut and voices everywhere are calling for an attack on the evils and injustices of our own world. But Columbus did more for Europe by sailing westward than whole generations of men who stayed behind. True, we must rebuild our cities and our societies, and bind up the wounds we have inflicted upon Mother Earth. To do this, we will need all the marvelous new tools of space—the weather and communications and resources satellites that are about to transform the economy of mankind. Even with their aid, it will be a difficult and often discouraging task, with little glamour to fire the imagination.

Yet, "where there is no vision, the people perish." Men need the mystery and romance of new horizons almost as badly as they need food and shelter. In the difficult years ahead, we should remember that the Snows of Olympus lie silent beneath the stars, waiting for our grandchildren.

These words were written in 1973, soon after the Apollo program had been terminated.* I am happy to say that they are even more timely now than they were twelve years ago, and much of the credit for this goes to Senator Spark Matsunaga. His advocacy of space exploration is singularly appropriate, because his beautiful state contains Earth's nearest rival to the Martian Mount Olympus. Although the summit of Mauna Kea is nearly three miles above sea level, its *real* height is six miles, measured from the bottom of the Pacific. And since there are no oceans on Mars, this is the only fair way of comparing the two giant volcanoes.

When Senator Matsunaga wrote to me in 1984, suggesting that I give my views on international space cooperation to the Senate Committee on Foreign Relations, Mars had already been on my agenda for fifty years. I remembered how, as a schoolboy in the early thirties, I'd managed during my lunch hour to devour Wells's *The War of the Worlds* in hasty installments at a local bookstore. Around the same time, I discovered the Mars novels of Edgar Rice Burroughs; later came the astronomer Percival Lowell—whose Mars, we now know, is quite as fabulous as E.R.B.'s.

And in due course I was to start my own literary career with *The Sands of Mars* (1951). A quarter of a century later, I would be distinctly embarrassed by one statement in the novel: "There are no mountains on Mars." But the title has been triumphantly vindicated; Mariner 9 showed vast deserts ridged with splendid sand dunes.

As it turned out, I was unable to appear at the Senate Foreign

---

* *"The Snows of Olympus" was originally published in* Playboy *magazine (December 1974); the full version can be found in* The View from Serendip. *Now that its real nature has been discovered, Nix Olympica has been renamed Mons Olympica. It is a safe bet that any snows on its summit will be of carbon dioxide, rather than water.*

Relations Committee Hearing, because the Pontifical Academy of Science was holding a space conference later that same month (September 1984). Fortunately, modern technology enables one to be in any number of places at the same time, so I made my presentation on videotape. This is how I concluded my fifteen-minute address, "A Martian Odyssey":*

Though unmanned space missions are essential and often highly cost-effective, they do not fire the imagination. And, contrary to what some scientists may have told you, in the long run it is the *manned* missions that will be the more important. Unfortunately, no one can predict whether that run will last for centuries, or mere decades. Almost certainly it will exceed the attention span of even the most enlightened Administration.

I have just been listening to an historic and inspiring sound from the past—the applause of Congress as President Kennedy cried "We choose to go to the Moon!" One day the United States will return to the Moon. That will be exciting and important; but it will no longer be pioneering. The Moon, though an essential stepping-stone to space, is only the offshore island of Earth. But Mars—a planet as large as our own, in terms of land area—is the first of the New Worlds.

In just a few years, it will be exactly half a millennium since three tiny ships sailed forth from Spain, to change the history of our species. And three is about right for the smallest practical Mars expedition—one unmanned cargo vessel, and two manned ships, either able to carry both crews in an emergency . . .

So is it absurdly optimistic to hope that, by Columbus Day 1992, the United States and the Soviet Union will have emerged from their long winter of sterile confrontation? That would be none too soon to start talking seriously about Mankind's next, and greatest, adventure.

* *See* Congressional Record, *13 September 1984, pp. 59–63.*

When we said goodbye in Star Village, Alexei Leonov—who is a very good artist—gave me a copy of his book *Life among Stars*. In it are the sketches he made during the Apollo–Soyuz mission, including excellent likenesses of his American colleagues.

The portrait of Tom Stafford is autographed as follows: "To my dear friend Alexei Leonov—many thanks for your friendship and wonderful co-operation—we have opened a new Era in the history of man. Tom Stafford, 18 July 1975." General Stafford—over to you . . .

And now, as you will see from this book, Senator Matsunaga has taken up the challenge.

Spark—over to you.

Arthur C. Clarke

Colombo, Sri Lanka
18 August 1985

ONE

GLIMPSES OF A NEW AGE

1 / TWO VISIONS

Huge white domes stand among the cinder cones atop the tallest island mountain in the Pacific, Mauna Kea. High above the clouds, the telescopes under these domes scan the heavens. At an altitude of 13,600 feet and a latitude near the equator, far removed from the lights of civilization, the dormant volcano Mauna Kea has emerged as the finest astronomical site in the world. Here on Hawaii's "Big Island" the stars can be studied under ideal conditions.

The nine telescopes in place or under preparation belong to the United States, Canada, France, Great Britain, the Netherlands, and Japan. They include two telescopes that will be larger than any others in the world—a 7.5-meter Japanese telescope; and an $80 million 10-meter American facility (four times larger than the famous observatory at Mt. Palomar), to be built jointly by the California Institute of Technology and the University of California.

On my first visit to the observatory complex in 1980, my guide was Dr. John Jefferies, director of the University of Hawaii's Institute for Astronomy, a dynamic Australian who almost single-handedly made Mauna Kea a world center under his institute's management. We stopped first at the base camp at nine thousand feet. Jefferies led me into a cafeteria where astronomers from four continents were finishing their midday breakfast after a night of stargazing and a morning's sleep. I was struck by their appearance as they sat hunched over steaming mugs of coffee. With their blue jeans, flannel shirts, boots, and a better than average number of beards, they might have been workers in a logging camp. Yet most of them were astrophysicists from leading universities throughout the world. They had been drawn to this unlikely site—this giant snowcapped mountain in the middle of the Pacific Ocean—by a shared commitment to the cosmos itself.

I was anxious to talk to them, learn from them. I recalled how, in 1975, three American astronauts and two Russian cosmonauts had guided their separate Apollo and Soyuz spacecraft to a linkup in space, and the world cheered as the cold war briefly gave way before a higher purpose. Could it happen again on a more sustained basis? What opportunities did the heavens offer for reaching beyond the cold war?

Pulling up a chair, I sat down alongside a French scientist and began our conversation by asking his impression of the Apollo–Soyuz mission. He answered matter-of-factly: "For the general public, it was inspiring to see adversaries working together in space, but for space scientists, it was nothing new. Although our cooperative activities may seem modest to an outsider, they are often extremely complex, and what we can do is limited mainly by the policies of national governments."

"But surely," I said, "language, nationalism, and political differences can be almost insurmountable barriers even among yourselves."

"Senator," the Frenchman replied, "the world is full of differences, but even more numerous are the similarities. For politicians, the world is many divided communities. But scientists belong to one community. We all speak the same language—the international language of science. And we share the same goals. If an astronomer in Chile or Canada discovers a new star, astronomers everywhere benefit equally."

Later, we boarded Land-Rovers for the bone-crushing drive up a road carved out of black volcanic rock to the summit more than four thousand feet above. We drove up through the clouds onto a rocky plateau. Scattered before us, like temples of a lost civilization, were the gleaming white observatories manned by scientists of many nations.

"We all speak the same language here . . . We share the same goals . . ."

Memories of that visit to the summit of Mauna Kea have never been far from my thoughts. They stand in sharp contrast to the political world I inhabit. I have no illusions about the international scientific community. Like everyone else, scientists are prone to rivalries and petty jealousies. Nevertheless, they still feel the powerful unifying pull of a common language and shared goals.

For a practical politician, their unity holds a special appeal. It isn't romantic idealism that unites scientists from different nations and cultures. They don't think of their activities as an Experiment in International Living. They aren't trying to "build bridges of intercultural communication." They're too busy for any of that. And yet, merely by pursuing a profession whose very character is international, they have created something that politicians seek in vain or reject as impossibly idealistic—a working community that transcends national borders.

And for space scientists, there is something more—the sheer physical vastness of their subject, its awesome mystery and grandeur. The cosmic laboratory of the space scientist is a frontier such as humanity has never known. Here science and advancing civilization intersect in full view of the world. Together they face a challenge so immense, so complex, that it's almost beyond belief.

There will be no lone adventurers—no Kit Carsons or Daniel Boones—in space. Instead, the model space frontiersman will participate in a mammoth scientific and technical enterprise. Civilization will be carried into space by many people working together on a scale never before achieved.

At first, I saw no way to act on those reflections. The prospect they offered seemed so remote from my daily whirl of activity—committee hearings on the budget, taxes, foreign trade, congressional strategy sessions, meetings with constituents, official receptions, lunches, dinners—in which the future is measured in hours and minutes and policy-making is dominated by the crisis at hand. Building bridges to a new future in space seemed beyond the scope of everyday politics, an impossible dream.

But the dream persisted, in part because of a guilty awareness that the chief stumbling block to its realization appeared to be my own political world. Somehow we had to find a way to develop policies that reached beyond our daily concerns to tap the unique potential of space. If we didn't, we would destroy that potential before we even had a chance to take advantage of it.

Fortunately, I thought, there was still plenty of time to encourage cooperative policies. The Space Age was only just beginning. At a certain point, perhaps in the next century, the common goals and challenges of the space frontier would grow into an irresistible force for unified action.

So I pondered the issue without any great sense of urgency until the summer of 1982, when a constituent sent me an article from an aerospace journal. The article dealt with the potential for constructing laser battle stations in space. The battle stations would be placed in near-earth orbit and targeted on Soviet missile silos. According to the author, the Russians were planning laser battle stations and the United States would be well advised to do the same.

The vision I had nurtured privately, which provided some consolation in the worsening climate of the cold war on earth, suddenly seemed threatened. If space became yet another East–West battleground, the path to a new age in space would be closed. I asked my staff to research the issue. They turned up a growing literature—albeit limited to technical journals far removed from the mainstream of public discussion—which envisioned new generations of weapons for space. Rather than having our nation's scientific genius lead a creative international effort to explore the cosmos, these writers sought to mobilize the scientific community to use space for yet another cycle of sterile confrontation. Instead of pointing outward to new worlds, scientists would design laser battle stations that would point deadly weapons back toward earth.

But perhaps the advocates of laser battle stations didn't fully appreciate the opportunities they might be foreclosing. I decided to write an article that described the path to a new era in space and offered a means to keep it open. The article appeared in *The Washington Post* on July 4, 1982. It began:

Our best—and perhaps last—opportunity to reach a workable accommodation with the Soviets appears on the verge of being lost before it is properly recognized.

While disarmament talks and negotiations must necessarily continue, the greatest opportunity appears to lie not in the narrow confines of a conference room but in the reaches of space. Within this decade, the United States and the Soviet Union plan to build permanent manned space stations. The age of space colonization, which scientists say will be comparable to the time when life emerged from the sea to colonize the land, will have begun.

But why two hostile space stations? Space—the last and most expansive frontier—will be what we make it. Must we make it into another "real world" living on the brink of self-annihilation? Must we play the same old unwinnable game in space, too?

The article went on to propose that the first permanently manned space station be developed as an international project. It concluded:

A joint project in space would add a refreshingly expansive dimension to life on a planet edging toward self-annihilation.

The arms buildup on planet earth could continue—Trident, MX, CX, B-l, RDF, whatever our hearts desire . . . But meanwhile, we also would be working on something with the Soviets. Something big. Something daring, bearing hope for the future.

And if it catches on, if we actually build some common ground up there, begin seeding it, wouldn't it be worth a try? . . .

Soon afterward, I sent copies of my article to the White House and the Departments of State and Defense for comment. Everyone wondered what I was worried about. Defense Secretary Caspar Weinberger wrote that a space arms race wasn't in the offing. Dr. George Keyworth, the President's Science Adviser, replied that the Soviets wouldn't want to cooperate with us; and even if they did, "we would lose more than we would gain." Both men also wrote that the Soviets were working on space weapons. If true, did that mean we intended to let them deploy weapons in space without responding? Of course not.

It seemed clear to me that, in typical fashion, we were backing into a new phase in the arms race. We would wait until the Soviet program was well underway; then, in an atmosphere of crisis, with "national survival" at stake, we would launch a crash program to catch up. No doubt we would succeed, as we had always done in the past. But meanwhile we would have passed beyond the point of no return. We would be trapped in a new spiraling of space-weapons competition, each country successively and endlessly producing counterweapons. It would be as dangerous as a breeder reactor running out of control.

How could we begin to move toward a more hopeful vision? I was sure the community of space scientists would have some ideas.

8

But there was no time to consult them during the hectic closing days of the 1982 Congress, before we left for the campaign trail. Still, I decided in September at least to place my concerns on record by submitting a resolution describing the danger and offering an alternative.

The resolution began: "Whereas the United States and the Soviet Union are on a course leading toward an arms race in space which is in the interest of no one . . ." It concluded by inviting the President to "initiate talks with the Government of the Soviet Union, and with other interested governments of countries having a space capability, with a view toward exploring the possibilities for a weapons-free international space station as an alternative to competing armed space stations."*

In my remarks on the Senate floor accompanying introduction of the resolution near the end of September, I sketched out an initial rationale for making space cooperation a foreign-policy objective, complementing arms-control negotiations and weapons buildup, as one means of influencing the evolution of events in space. "Surely the concept is worth exploring," I said. "Surely we owe that much to future generations. Allowing space to become an arena of conflict without first exerting every effort to make it into an arena of cooperation would amount to an abdication of governmental responsibility that would never be forgotten."

The joint space-station resolution was ignored in the closing rush of business. Even the media in my home state, which usually reported new initiatives from their representatives in Washington, found this one too far-out to mention. An arms race in space? Absurd.

But I wasn't so sure. In any event, it was clear to me that steps had to be taken to encourage greater space cooperation and alert

* The text of this resolution, and of succeeding space cooperation resolutions, can be found in the Appendix.

the American people to its potential. A space station—national or international—was still a long way off. But perhaps other promising space science activities might be initiated at once. As I returned to Hawaii for the election campaign, I made a note to consult the space scientists there. This time, I had some very practical objectives in mind.

2 / THE SPACE-TIME DIMENSION

In December 1982, after the people of Hawaii returned me to office and before traveling to Washington for the new session of Congress, I contacted David Morrison, a member of the faculty of the University of Hawaii's Institute for Astronomy that oversaw activities on Mauna Kea. A brilliant young Harvard-educated astrophysicist, Morrison was especially qualified to lay out the opportunities for space science cooperation. His many professional activities included chairmanship of the national Solar System Exploration Committee (SSEC for short, and pronounced "seek"), a blue-ribbon panel established by NASA in 1980 to chart a long-term national program for planetary exploration. Morrison testified frequently at congressional hearings and briefings, where he displayed a superb talent for making the cosmos comprehensible. I telephoned him, told him of my concerns. With his usual efficiency and enthusiasm, he offered to brief me the following day.

The secretary in my Honolulu office barely had a chance to announce him before SSEC's irrepressible chairman came into the room, a slide projector cradled in his arms. "Senator Matsunaga," he said, "I've brought a SSEC presentation that I think will serve as the best basis for discussion."

"Then let's begin at once," I said, and without any preliminary chitchat, I drew the curtains while he set up the projector. On his signal, I turned off the light and the first image lit up the wall opposite my desk.

NASA Planetary Exploration through the Year 2000.
Recommendations of the Solar System Exploration
Committee.

The first slide introduced an illuminating series, narrated by my buoyant instructor, describing the exciting history of planetary exploration, its current sorry state, and SSEC's proposals for a dramatic revival. I was surprised to learn from his presentation that, since the mid-1970s, our planetary exploration program had been virtually grounded. What Morrison called the "golden age" of planetary exploration occurred between 1962 and 1978. During that period, the United States launched some forty robot spacecraft toward the moon and distant planets, including the Mariner series to Venus, Mercury, and Mars; the two Pioneers to Jupiter, Saturn, and beyond: Voyagers 1 and 2 to Jupiter and Saturn; the stunning pair of Viking probes to Mars which landed on the surface of the red planet and sent back streams of color photographs . . .

"It's hard to realize," Morrison explained, "but in a little more than a decade we have created a whole new cosmic context for life on earth. We weren't just launching spacecraft. We were launching a new age!"

At that point, I interrupted him. "Dave, I have a confession to make about those space missions. People who know better than I do keep saying they are important and I believe them. But I still find it very hard to be concerned. Frankly, whether or not there is nitrogen or hydrogen on Venus or Jupiter doesn't excite me very much.'

"You are not alone, Senator," Dave replied, "you're just a victim of instant-information overload, a common disease. It prevents people from perceiving the big picture. For instance, the greatest contribution of the Space Age may be that it will cure us of future shock. We will learn how to look at accelerated change, and live with it, in new and more relaxed ways. What space scientists call long lead times—big blocks of years—will be an accepted part of our daily perceptions and activities.

"We'll initiate projects that we *know* won't be completed in our lifetime; but we will accept that way of seeing things. In fact, that's really the way life is. Our perception of time is incredibly narrow and out of joint. The Space Age will synchronize our thinking with the rhythmic patterns of life itself. It will permanently alter the way we perceive both time and space. Everything will appear in a new light. If only the politicians don't blow us up first." He paused and with an embarrassed smile began shuffling through his stack of slides. His enthusiasm had carried him further than he intended. And I was glad for it.

"Dave," I said, "I've been in politics long enough to know its limitations. Politicians deal with what we call a 'real world' that is limited by established patterns of thought and action. Every age has its governing 'real world.' It rules as long as it works. When 'real world' solutions only seem to perpetuate the problem, it's time to look to new frontiers. Keep talking."

Dave went on to describe the climactic events of the "golden age," the Viking and Voyager missions. The two Vikings were launched to Mars in the summer of 1975 and landed on the red planet a year later. The two Voyagers catapulted into space in August and September of 1977. In September 1981, Voyager 1 completed the seventy-million-mile trip to Jupiter and began transmitting data back to earth. The messages streamed into the Voyager Mission Control Center at the Jet Propulsion Laboratory in Pasadena; scientists from around the world had come to California for the historic event. For the Americans there, the celebration

13

was also something of a wake. With the exception of a pair of four-to-six-month probes to Venus, no spacecraft had been launched by the United States since the two Voyagers in 1977. Shortly before the 1981 reunion in Pasadena, the United States decided against building an American spacecraft for the international fleet that would be launched toward Halley's comet in 1984 and 1985. As five coordinated spacecraft from the U.S.S.R., Europe, and Japan converged on Halley's comet in the spring of 1986, the United States would watch from the sidelines.*

Morrison explained that SSEC was established in 1980 to revive the U.S. planetary exploration program. The program had faltered in large measure because of the demands that development of the space shuttle had placed on NASA's resources. Already, funding for planetary activities had nosedived to twenty percent of the mid-1970s level. SSEC's job was to plan a low-cost long-term program for planetary exploration that could survive the ups and downs of NASA's budget. Dave's committee first came up with bargain-basement designs for two spacecraft that could be built with off-the-shelf technology.

With the means of transportation decided, the committee turned to targets in the solar system, beginning with a core program, which Dave quickly summarized: For the inner planets (Venus, Mars, Earth, and its moon), three priority missions: (1) map the surface of Venus, using an orbiting spacecraft that would also collect geophysical data; (2) orbit Mars for two years, collecting data on the planet's surface chemistry and climate; (3) orbit the moon for the same purposes as Mars. For the outer planets (Jupiter, Saturn, Uranus, Neptune): send an orbiter to Saturn and a probe into the atmosphere of its moon Titan, as a successor to the Galileo spacecraft under design for a long-delayed mission to Jupiter which

---

* Later we caught up with our error and diverted a spacecraft from another mission to approach another comet (although at a much greater distance than the Halley fleet and without their specifically designed equipment), and we also contributed NASA's Deep Space Tracking Network to the enterprise. Still, compared to the others, ours was a face-saving, catch-up role.

14

scientists hoped would be launched in 1988. To study the asteroids (solar-system bodies from a few feet to several hundred miles in diameter) and the vapor-tailed comets, the plan was to send a spacecraft close to the nucleus of a comet, with instruments that would record its properties, following a route that passed through an asteroid belt.

Dave also described other missions to Mars, asteroids, comets, Saturn, and Uranus, for a total of fourteen "assembly line" launches between 1988 and 2000.

"Well, Senator, what do you think?"

"David, it all seems very challenging and imaginative. But I must remind you of a partner in these stirring adventures whom you seem to have overlooked—the American taxpayer. What will all this cosmic voyaging cost?"

With a smile, he inserted a slide into the projector, and a chart appeared on the wall. Dave summarized: "As you know, NASA's budget runs about $7 billion a year. The core program that SSEC proposes would use less than five percent of NASA's budget, or $300 million annually. We don't think that's extravagant, considering that we would be the only ones exploring the planets. Neither the shuttle nor the space station, if it's ever built, will reach higher than a few hundred miles. Some of our probes will reach out several hundred *million* miles?"

"You don't sound very gung ho about a space station," I interjected.

"Senator, for nearly a decade of shuttle development, planetary scientists have scrambled for crumbs. Now, when the shuttle finally becomes operational, along comes space-station development to consume NASA's budget all over again. Can you blame us for being less than enthusiastic?"

I could see my international space station wouldn't get very far with the scientific community. They would probably suspect the idea was hatched by NASA to lure their support. (Subsequent interviews more than confirmed that impression.) Perhaps the solid

15

yet more modest SSEC program would be the best place to start.

"David," I said, "since your priorities are so dominated by financial considerations, to what extent have you considered working with other nations, the way astronomers work together on Mauna Kea?"

Dave seemed to have anticipated the question. He first pointed out that the space vehicles used on scientific missions generally fall into four categories:

1. *Fly-by* reconnaissance spacecraft, the easiest to design and build, which direct their instruments at a planet while flying past it

2. *Orbiters* that go into orbit around a planet for an extended period

3. *Entry probes* or *landers*, usually released by an orbiter, which penetrate the atmosphere of a planet and sometimes are programmed to land on its surface, as Viking did on Mars.

4. *Sample collectors,* unmanned "sample return" missions, which land, collect samples of soil and rock, then return them to earth.

Sample-return missions offer the highest scientific yield, but they're also the most expensive. Our only sample-return missions were part of the manned Apollo program, when astronauts brought back rocks from the moon. The only fully automated sample-return mission was conducted by the U.S.S.R., from the moon also. Although sample returns are the first choice of all planetary scientists, their cost prevented SSEC from considering any for its core program. A sample return from Mars, the top choice of the international planetary science community, would cost an estimated $3 billion spread over a ten-year period of design and development.

"Obviously," said Morrison, "the more expensive the mission, the more it makes sense to share the cost with other nations, especially when you can't afford to do it on your own. We have an extensive and growing joint program with Canada and the eleven members of ESA (the European Space Agency). ESA is spending $1 billion to build the Spacelab for our shuttle and ESA countries frequently design instruments and experiments for our planetary science missions.

"But launch costs count the most. At the moment, only two nations have interplanetary launch capabilities—we and the Soviet Union.* We had a program of cooperation with the Soviets that seemed to be making headway. It was carried out under a five-year space cooperation agreement negotiated by Nixon and Brezhnev in 1972 and renewed in 1977. But when the agreement came up for renewal earlier this year, the United States pulled out."

"I realize that," I said, "and I know we declined to renew it in reaction to martial law in Poland. If the agreement hadn't automatically come up for renewal at that moment, it might still be in effect. Besides Apollo–Soyuz, what other less well known activities were sponsored by the agreement?"

"Few people outside the scientific community realize how valuable that cooperation was for American scientists. There were conferences, data exchanges, advice on missions, which helped us immensely. In 1971, for example, the Soviets launched two unmanned missions to Mars. Each was a combined orbiter and lander. Both orbited successfully. The first lander reportedly crashed. The second landed successfully, but after about twenty seconds communication with it was lost; it may have been overwhelmed by a dust storm. The Soviets launched two more Mars missions in 1973, again with limited success.

"But they obtained an immense amount of operational data from those four missions, especially on the problems spacecraft encounter during the descent to the Martian surface and on choosing landing sites. They made that information available to us under the space cooperation agreement, and it helped us considerably in designing our subsequent Viking missions to Mars. Politically, it was unwise

---

* Since that meeting with Dave Morrison in 1982, ESA and Japan have acquired comparatively modest interplanetary launch capabilities.

17

for the Soviets to help us succeed where they had failed. But they respected the terms of the agreement and international scientific cooperation won out."

"Dave," I said, "Congress needs to hear more of the information you just gave me. If I introduced a resolution to renew the space cooperation agreement, would the scientific community support it with expert testimony?"

"I wouldn't pretend to speak for everyone. But I think there's a consensus that canceling the agreement did not serve American interests. As for testimony, there are other scientists who have worked more closely than I with the Soviets. They're more qualified to testify. I'll send you a list."

After Dave left, I opened the window blinds and paused to look out on Honolulu harbor. In a berth directly across from my office, a turn-of-the-century three-masted cargo vessel rested at anchor, its sails reefed; a line of visitors filed past a makeshift box office and onto the gangplank. *Falls of Clyde* was painted in large white lettering on its stern. In another era, it had carried sugar and pineapples to California and returned with passengers and every kind of cargo. Now it was a floating museum. Could any of the ship's passengers in 1900 have possibly imagined that in a few decades people would travel between California and Hawaii in four and a half hours in a Boeing 747? Could I possibly imagine today how people would be traveling in 2060?

Indeed, I could. Seventy-five years from now, "if the politicians don't blow us up first," earth's inhabitants will travel deep into space aboard rocket ships whose design principles are already well known. One of my great-grandchildren might work, perhaps even settle, on a distant planet that had been mapped by a SSEC core-program mission. It's merely a matter of time.

Time and space. Dave Morrison had carefully outlined what most of us only vaguely surmise. Technology narrowed our perceptions of space; it accustomed us to think in shorter time frames as we moved quickly from the horse and buggy to automobiles to jet aircraft. And as that happened, the size of our planet seemed to shrink.

Contemporary policies based on perceptions of rapid change and shrinking space will be directly challenged by the very long distances and lead times required for Space Age activity. Missions will take years and perhaps even generations to complete. The far distant future will acquire an immediacy it now lacks. Meanwhile, our sense of space will both expand and become more embracing. In an earlier age, Columbus discovered America, then others mapped it. In the future, orbiters and landers will map planets *before* humans arrive—we will first see new worlds in their unified wholeness. Our sense of time and space will change dramatically. Technology, which has divided us from the rhythms of nature, will reunite us with them and give us a new dimension of perception.

Time and space. I hadn't thought seriously about such concepts since I studied college physics. Cooperate with the Russians in space? Only if it served our interests. But how could we know our interests in the Space Age if we did not first try to understand its unique character and requirements?

3 / SCIENCE, ART, AND ASTRONAUTS

Dave Morrison had provided me with a list of scientist-experts on Soviet space activities, plus a stack of documents he calls my "space studies homework." I set to work on the return flight to Washington, cruising at 37,000 feet above the Pacific where the *Falls of Clyde* had once sailed, and considering proposals to work in space with the Russians. What was I getting into? From my politician's "real world" perspective, it seemed wholly unreal. But when I shifted my perspective, the Space Age acquired an impending reality that dwarfed everything else. The challenge was to see and work with the two realities at once, and develop policies that connected them.

My homework included a report of the Committee on Planetary and Lunar Exploration, or COMPLEX, a blue-ribbon panel organized by the National Academy of Sciences, under the chairmanship of Professor Gerald J. Wasserburg of the California Institute of Technology. David Morrison's SSEC had been created to define specific missions. COMPLEX assumed the broader task of developing an overall policy into which SSEC's missions would be incorporated. Whereas SSEC was inspired by past experiences with the politics of NASA and Congress, COMPLEX looked toward the unfolding policy requirements of a future age.

Given the scope and cost of space exploration, COMPLEX concluded that, at the minimum, missions of spacefaring nations should be coordinated, so as to avoid duplication, reduce and share costs, and maximize scientific return. Ultimately, many missions would be most profitably undertaken as joint enterprises. Any other long-term space policy would be wasteful in the extreme. For planetary exploration, a planetary perspective was imperative.

Next, COMPLEX examined the space activities of the only two nations then capable of launching interplanetary probes, the U.S. and the U.S.S.R., and concluded that their planetary programs were remarkably complementary. For instance, the U.S. had relied on the astronauts of the Apollo program to collect geological samples from the moon. Meanwhile, the Soviets had pioneered in robot vehicles that roamed the moon's surface and gathered samples. After the Apollo program went out of the business in 1972, resourceful American scientists developed refined instruments for conducting geological measurements of the moon at great distances from orbiting spacecraft. A logical next step would be to use our operational orbiters to select landing sites for the Russians' operational landers, with both countries sharing the scientific findings.

A parallel situation existed for Venus, where we were analyzing the atmosphere with orbiters and the Soviets were using landers to study its surface. The Soviet Venus program included fourteen missions to that planet through 1984, far more than we had planned. Coordinating future missions would make "no direct impact on the independent operation of the two exploration programs," COMPLEX noted. It would merely "allow investigations to be carried out at a depth and quality that is beyond the foreseeable means of either nation alone and that provides economies on both sides."

Even in the context of the most narrow self-interest, COMPLEX concluded that cooperation was the desirable policy. While the space exploration programs of the U.S., Europe, and Japan were conducted on an open basis, with scientific findings available to anyone who sought them, the Soviets were often slow to divulge what they learned without a formal exchange agreement. The choice was between bringing light to Soviet darkness or keeping ourselves in the dark about what they were doing. COMPLEX had made the most rational, self-interested choice.

One other COMPLEX conclusion made a strong impression on me: "There is an element of risk for any nation that may wish to cooperate with the United States in space exploration, because of the process by which space missions are defined and approved." COMPLEX was delicately referring to the political process in Washington. Space missions required *long lead times:* the most modest interplanetary probe required a reliable and steady five-to-ten-year commitment. Yet federal budgets were planned on a year-to-year basis and acted upon on a day-to-day or even minute-to-minute basis. COMPLEX pointed out that even among democratic nations the United States experienced unique difficulty in developing long-term space activities.

Both the U.S. and the U.S.S.R., then, had problems with long lead times and they seemed oddly complementary. Soviet leaders had the advantage of pursuing long-term planning without concern for shifting political moods; but the Soviet bureaucracy was slow and inefficient. We enjoyed the advantage of flexibility and the efficiencies of a competitive economy; but we had a hard time with sustained long-term planning. Perhaps, in addition to meeting the Soviet challenge, we ought also to consider how democratic institutions might best cope with the unprecedented requirements of space exploration. Ultimately, that response could determine whether democracy prevails in the Space Age.

Back in Washington in January, I got in touch with the scientists on Dave Morrison's list, told them of my plans to introduce a resolution calling for renewal of the U.S.–U.S.S.R. space cooperation agreement, and requested their views. I realized that what seemed most obvious to the scientific community might seem least obvious to the political community—namely, that America might actually benefit from cooperation with the Soviets. Too many American policymakers had slipped into the complacent belief that the Russians had severely limited space capabilities, a mistake that Sputnik should have corrected but didn't. I needed authoritative opinion, in writing.

Among those responding to my inquiries was Donald "Deke" Slayton, space entrepreneur, retired Air Force pilot, and former astronaut who had flown on the Apollo–Soyuz mission. One paragraph in Slayton's letter of endorsement, referring to Apollo–Soyuz, was especially revealing: "The proposition that we gave away technology [during Apollo–Soyuz] does not recognize the openness with which NASA conducts its business. Everything done is in the public domain and is available internationally to any interested party. Conversely, the U.S.S.R. program has been conducted under a heavy veil of secrecy and for the first time was open to public scrutiny. In my opinion, the major thing the Soviets could have learned, to their everlasting benefit, is how to conduct major technical programs efficiently through use of free lateral and vertical communications among all participants. This would also have been to our major benefit because it is called 'democracy.' Unfortunately, they have not opted to purloin these lessons yet, but we should not give up hope."

Besides debunking the myth that Apollo–Soyuz was a technology giveaway, Slayton had offered two important insights. First, he pointed out, as had others involved in Apollo–Soyuz, that the great advantage of cooperation for us was its inherent openness. When we cooperated, we knew and could control whatever information the Russians obtained; and, equally important, we could demand information in return. Second, the *process* of Apollo–Soyuz was democratizing. It moved methodically toward a predictable outcome and in so doing pushed the Soviets' closed system toward

23

greater openness at the points where we came into contact with it.

Dr. Thomas Donahue of the University of Michigan, chairman of the Space Science Board of the National Academy of Sciences, was, along with "Deke" Slayton, one of the first to reply to my query: "As a scientist who has participated in the Apollo–Soyuz mission and has been involved directly in scientific exchanges with the U.S.S.R. relating to the exploration of the planet Venus, I wish to express my enthusiastic support for the bill you are introducing on cooperation in space. Science flourishes best when it is conducted in an atmosphere of free and open exchange of data, analysis and criticism. In the case of the planetary exploration program, our experience in the past is that planetary science as a whole benefited greatly from the period of open exchange and cooperation with our colleagues in the U.S.S.R. Data obtained by our Pioneer Venus Orbiter was used to determine the proper landing sites for the probes Venera 13 and 14 and the future probes Venera 15 and 16. The data they obtained were thereby rendered much more meaningful to the great benefit of us as well as them. Failure to cooperate in this way means a great loss for science . . ."

The endorsements from Donahue's colleagues were equally emphatic. Dr. Eugene Levy, a planetary scientist from the University of Arizona, who was then directing cooperation negotiations with West European scientists, wrote: "The United States is not alone in its abilities to carry out solar system investigations. Other nations have developed similar interests as well as similar and complementary technical capabilities. Our ability to exploit these capabilities and interests for our own benefit and for the broader benefit of mankind would be enhanced greatly by the pooling of selected resources in solar system science . . ."

The phrase that stood out was "complementary technical capabilities." Again and again, that point was made by the experts. The solar system was so vast that no single nation could begin to address every relevant aspect of its exploration at once. It almost seemed as if the two chief space powers, the U.S. and the U.S.S.R., had unconsciously divided up the best initial opportunities. Now, as the two programs evolved, exciting new opportunities for benefiting from each other's expertise were beginning to appear. Levy continued: "During the past decade, attempts were made to initiate substantive collaboration with the Soviet Union in scientific exploration of the planets. . . . Having served as a member of the U.S. National Aeronautics and Space Administration delegation to the last of these talks, it was my distinct impression that important progress was being made and that we were on the verge of being able to strike modest, but still substantial, agreements, to cooperate in further exploration of the planet Venus. In the middle of this important progress, the Administration let these bilateral agreements lapse, thus terminating the discussion."

Thus, in the spring of 1982, just as the slow effort to reach agreement on Venus was on the verge of success, with its promise of major benefits for the United States, the United States government had refused to renew the space cooperation agreement. In order to "punish" the Soviets for their behavior in Poland, we sent them a "signal" on Venus. An inappropriate policy of "linkage" had made us administrators of coincidences. No vision, no anticipation—simply react, using whatever tool happened to be handy.

Herman Wouk, the celebrated author of *Winds of War,* called that process a "closed loop of insanity." He described it in an article on U.S.–U.S.S.R. relations he wrote for *Parade* magazine. The article appeared on February 6, 1983, at the time of my exchanges with planetary scientists. Impulsively, I wrote to Herman Wouk, shared my concerns, and enclosed a draft of the new resolution. He replied immediately:

We joined forces with the Russians in the Second World War to eliminate the Axis menace to civilized life on earth. We achieved that aim without resolving our ideological differences or even discussing them. The menace confronting us was enough to make us cooperate.

Now we and the Soviet peoples are confronted with a

menace to our survival more grave than Hitler's Axis. The menace is ourselves; our worser selves, frozen in suspicion, mistrust, and ideological antagonisms. Space offers us a fleeting chance to get away from the earthbound framework of confrontation and mistrust and join forces again. The Soviet Union is a great nation, however profoundly we disagree with its ideology and its leadership. We Americans, confident in our strength and our free way of life, can hold out our hand to the Soviets for cooperation in space, as a start toward saving our children from the deadly peril created by our mutual old fears, reflected in the arms control deadlock.

Your initiative in the matter of East–West cooperation is thoughtful, cautious, and promising. I support your Resolution and hope the Senate will endorse it.

Who was to blame for that closed loop of insanity? Their side? Our side? Of course, we were "right" in our reactions and the Soviets were "wrong" in the behavior that provoked us. But it was not enough to be right in a battle that only produced victories without hope. We were trapped in a process that consumed righteous and wicked alike.

Herman Wouk, novelist; Thomas Donahue and Eugene Levy, scientists; "Deke" Slayton, pilot-astronaut—each approached the issue from different perspectives, yet their conclusions converged. Wouk spoke with an artist's sensitivity of menacing undercurrents running deeper than ideology; Donahue and Levy described complementary activities on a new frontier; Slayton explained how cooperative pursuit of shared objectives on that frontier would permit democratic values to take the offensive. Each helped me realize how narrow my political perspective really was and how much government could still learn from the governed.

26

4 / SPACE WEAPONS
AND ARMS CONTROL

Early in March 1983, I assembled the notes from my interviews, correspondence, and reading and began sketching out a floor statement to accompany introduction of my congressional resolution calling for renewal of the U.S.–U.S.S.R. space cooperation agreement. Through the years, I had acquired the habit of working until three or four in the morning, or even later. Typically, there would be a reception in the evening (or two or three or four), after which I returned to a deserted office and tackled the mass of paperwork that had accumulated during a hectic Senate day. It was a pleasure to work alone and without interruption, fortified by hot tea sweetened with honey. During the day, thoughts formed instantly and faded just as fast, as I rushed from one activity to another. But at night, a thought could breathe a little, linger, until the imagination began to develop it.

It seemed to me that, from a legislative point of view, the space cooperation resolution was unique because of the special emphasis it placed on cooperation as a *foreign-policy objective* complementary to arms-control negotiations and weapons buildup. But in a nation

27

managed by lawyers trained in adversary proceeding (myself included) and businessmen schooled in tense competition, the *idea*
of cooperation inspired a certain uneasiness. We admired it in
principle, yet we were far more comfortable, innovative, and lively
when involved in an adversarial situation, be it in a congressional
hearing, a public debate, a battle for economic success, or the Super
Bowl. That raised an interesting question: To what extent were
our political attitudes and actions influenced by our culture's in-
clination toward adversary proceeding?

The space cooperation resolution was introduced on March 10,
1983, with Senator Claiborne Pell of Rhode Island, ranking Democrat on the Senate Foreign Relations Committee, as its cosponsor.
My floor statement attempted to develop a preliminary rationale
for a new cooperation policy that used democratic openness as a
force for change:

> Mr. President, I am today introducing, with the distinguished
> senior Senator from Rhode Island, Mr. Pell, a concurrent
> resolution, designed to encourage cooperative East–West ven-
> tures in space as an alternative to a space arms race. The
> resolution calls upon the President of the United States to
> renew the space cooperation agreement with the Soviet Union
> that brought a decade of benefits to American science and
> technology before it was allowed to lapse in 1982 . . .
>
> Mr. President, space cooperation agreements [and] control
> agreements involve very tough negotiating on both sides. The
> Soviets come in trying to take all they can get. Our space
> science negotiators, many of whom have at least as much
> experience negotiating with the Soviets as our arms control
> negotiators, and who have shown themselves to be as tough-
> minded as they come, refuse to budge until the Soviets adjust
> to reality. And the result so far—or at least until the space
> cooperation agreement was allowed to lapse—has been very
> much in the interest of the United States . . .
>
> For instance, as the Apollo–Soyuz timetable ticked off, the

Soviets opened up to an unprecedented extent. Scientists and technicians from both nations became wholly absorbed in the project, integrating distinctly different operational styles under the pressure of a shared deadline and a shared professional commitment to make the project work.

Thus, in mid-1973, an American delegation was admitted to the previously top secret Soviet mission control center—again, for the technically required purpose of coordinating communications and tracking. Looking out across the consoles, world maps, wall clocks, they saw, typed on a giant center screen: "Welcome American Colleagues."

The following year, American astronauts lived and trained at the Soviet space center outside Moscow, Soviet cosmonauts trained in Houston, and American public affairs officials successfully convinced the Russians to go on live TV.

Before the project concluded, on July 17, 1975, with a successful docking in space, the Soviets and Americans had negotiated and signed 133 working documents—an unprecedented achievement . . .

Under the technical imperatives generated by projects such as Apollo–Soyuz, the Soviets set a number of precedents for openness, information exchange, and verification, problems which have bedeviled our arms control negotiators for a generation. They did not do it willingly. The result was not a revolution in behavior, but it was an extremely promising beginning . . .

I ask my Senate colleagues to imagine what relations in this body would be like if Republicans and Democrats worked out of separate self-contained enclaves and met only over a negotiating table at irregular intervals. It's obvious: our differences would be exaggerated by an order of magnitude. Comparatively speaking, for the United States and the Soviet Union, we can speak of several orders of magnitude. It is a problem that cannot be alleviated by placing greater blame on one side or the other. If suspicion and mistrust are a Soviet disease, finding institutional expression in totalitarianism and repression, then we should be wary most of all of its contagion. And we should remind ourselves that the vaccine as well as the cure for that deadly disease happens to be a natural and extremely potent by-product of democratic society, decongealing cooperative activity, pursued with caution, with tough-mindedness, with sagacity, with prudence, yes; but still, pursued . . .

It is perhaps neither necessary nor desirable to begin with another dramatic Apollo–Soyuz. United States and Soviet planetary science objectives contain many opportunities for convergence that at once promise sound scientific achievement and point toward further collaboration across a discretely expanding front. But it is important always to keep in mind that our ultimate objective is to attain the unifying purposefulness and hope that offer the only sane way for human civilization to address the universe. Mr. President, the cold war does not need a new dimension. Allowing space to become an arena of conflict without first exerting every effort to make it into an arena of cooperation would constitute an abdication of the responsibilities of our office that would never be forgotten. I therefore call upon my colleagues to join with me in supporting this modest beginning for a grand design.

The resolution stirred little interest, in part because we were proposing cooperation as an alternative to a space arms race that seemed nowhere in sight. Then something quite unexpected occurred. On March 23, 1983, less than two weeks after the introduction of our resolution, President Reagan delivered a nationally televised address in which he presented a "vision of the future that offers hope." He called upon the American scientific community to build a Space Age weapons system that would make nuclear weapons "impotent and obsolete." Suddenly everyone was talking about Star Wars. Later the concept was formally named the Strategic Defense Initiative, or SDI. But the Star Wars title stuck.*

I respected the sincerity of space-weapons supporters, sympathized with their aspirations, often found myself at odds with their stand-pat critics. Appalled at the spiraling madness of the nuclear-arms race and disgusted with the limited success of arms control, they sought to transcend the whole thing. They were as fed up as I was with a suicidal process that seemed unable if not unwilling to reach outside itself. The prevailing nuclear doctrine, called MAD—mutually assured destruction—was mad indeed.

Unfortunately, space weapons, however well intentioned, don't treat the madness. The weapons of MAD are a product of a relationship that has evolved into a closed loop of insanity in which weapons of "offense" and "defense" are part of the same maddening process. Even if the Strategic Defense Initiative works to perfection and Soviet ICBMs are rendered "impotent," the disease will continue to spread: the Soviets will simply shift to other strategies of nuclear deployment even more mad than MAD.

The political philosopher Hannah Arendt called terrorism the explosion of impotence. By making the Soviet ICBM fleet impotent—by separating their nuclear weapons from any comprehensive strategy—we would open the door to an explosively anarchic age of nuclear terrorism. We would give the Soviets incentive to plant their "impotent" hydrogen bombs anywhere—in New York, say, or London—and perhaps even hold our entire Star Wars

---

* Supporters of space weapons were unhappy with the Star Wars image. "Space shield" was suggested as a cheerier alternative, but it didn't catch on either.

Then the leading space-weapons advocacy group, called High Frontier, developed a TV commercial, which was used in a nationwide campaign. It featured animated drawings of stick people, a dog, a house, and a sun, and the voice of a seven-year-old child actor from Boston. She asked her father what Star Wars was all about. A white arc appeared in the sky. Father explained that the arc was a peace shield that would stop bad missiles. The stick people smiled, the sun smiled, the arc turned into a rainbow. With a bow to both sides, I'll use both Star Wars and SDI. Either way, we're talking about space weapons and not rainbows.

system hostage. An "impotent" nuclear-armed Soviet Union would present us with problems that would make Middle East terrorism seem like a playful lark.

When the SDI concept was introduced, its proponents suggested that we might gradually guide the Soviets into a comparable commitment. But how could we expect to guide the Soviets anywhere when our *relationship* was poisoned by compulsive suspicion and mistrust? The idea that we could induce the cumbersome, secretive, paranoid Soviet regime to adopt a whole new military strategy and a new generation of weapons, based on our military's perceptions of what was best for their military, was the greatest fantasy of all.

Anyhow, I thought, at least the new focus on space will insure more serious attention for the space cooperation option embodied in my resolution. But I was mistaken. The space-weapons issue quickly became polarized along usual liberal-versus-conservative lines. Since my proposal was offered as an alternative to a space arms race, it was automatically assigned to the liberal camp. But with the strong exception of Claiborne Pell, liberals generally ignored it. Defense-reform liberals focused on reducing Star Wars funding. Arms-control liberals focused on space arms-control negotiations. Liberal scientist-experts focused on the mechanics of Star Wars, opposing it on the grounds that it wouldn't work. None of them showed much interest in cooperation as an alternative policy.

With no meaningful support from liberals or conservatives, my resolution became an orphan; it was denied a hearing and faded out of sight while the space-weapons debate raged on.

On arms-control issues, I invariably voted the liberal position, although I shared the discomfort of conservatives with an important aspect of it. I believed in negotiations, even with adversaries who could not be trusted—*especially* with them. Sure, they might cheat and take every advantage, but it was still worthwhile to keep pressing for verifiable negotiated solutions that protected our interests. Keep them at the table, keep talking, keep probing—it was the least we could do when the two rivals were aiming enough explosive power at each other to blow up the world.

But at the same time I was troubled by an evolution that seemed to be occurring within the arms-control process itself. As weapons systems proliferated and grew ever more complex, arms control entered an ever-deepening maze. How many Pershing IIs equalled how many SS-20s? Did a Soviet ICBM in a hardened silo in the Ukraine equal a Poseidon missile in an American submarine in the North Atlantic? The South Atlantic? How many B-52 bombers based in Guam equaled how many Backfire bombers based in Vladivostok? How many apples equaled five oranges? At 30 degrees longitude? In the winter? Between 5 and 6 p.m.? It was reaching a point where the most we could expect was a slowing down of the dizzying growth of the endless maze.

Along the way, the very nature of arms control changed. It was no longer merely a process. It had also become a profession. Federal agencies, universities, think tanks, plunged into those labyrinthine depths. Experts churned out reports, books, doctoral dissertations, learned articles, decipherable only by other maze dwellers or former maze dwellers who had graduated to endowed chairs in maze analysis at prominent universities. Foundations funded institutes for maze specialists to meet and discuss their findings, and conferences, seminars, weekend retreats on private estates. Arms-control specialists found it increasingly difficult to communicate their findings to the general public. More and more, they talked only to themselves—and to Soviet maze dwellers who prowled the same labyrinth.

Cooperation, on the other hand, is an inherently open process. The Soviets would, of course, try to exploit it by negotiating favorable arrangements. But we could always see what they were doing and deal with it. More important, once an agreed-upon project began, the Soviets couldn't cheat. Each side *had* to know what the other was doing or they would both fail. Did a pilot hide information from his co-pilot? The entire thrust of cooperation was toward ever greater openness and verification. It allowed American values and institutions to take the offensive.

Even as the space cooperation resolution sank out of sight, I grew more convinced than ever that it represented something new and worthwhile. People weren't so much against it as unable to *see* it because it existed outside familiar patterns of perception. Intellectually, it supported the arms-control position. Emotionally, it was stirred by the can-do spirit of SDI. Imaginatively, it seemed to be reaching for something beyond the debate. I found it an enlightening position from which to examine many of the political viewpoints I had taken for granted for so long.

TWO

OPENING THE PATH

5 / THE GREAT LOST OPPORTUNITY

During most of 1983, as the space-weapons debate intensified into a war of its own, I continued to look for ways in which a policy of space cooperation might be implemented. In order to avoid past mistakes, I sought to learn more about the history of U.S.–U.S.S.R. space activities. In the process I acquired a new appreciation of a remarkable event called the International Geophysical Year. The IGY, as it was called, actually ran for nearly two years, 1957 and 1958. It mobilized an army of sixty thousand scientists from sixty-six nations, including the U.S. and the U.S.S.R., to study planet Earth from pole to pole and from outer space. "The IGY," said Prince Philip of England, "is the world studying itself." Walter Sullivan, in his book *Assault on the Unknown,* described the scene on the eve of the July 1, 1957, initiation of IGY: "In preparation for this day, observers had been placed in the most remote parts of the earth—at the South Pole, on drifting floes near the North Pole, in huts perilously perched on mountaintops from Haut de Stalin, Bulgaria, to Mount Eva Perón, Argentina . . . Other scientists were on Mount Norikura, Japan; at Tunchuan Peak, New Mexico

37

. . . [There were] Americans in a tunnel at Dalton Canyon in California, Germans in a potash mine, and Italians in a grotto near Trieste . . ."

The fruits of the IGY exceeded even the most hopeful expectations. World Data Centers were established in the U.S., the U.S.S.R., and Europe, and information flowed through those connecting points as if through the neurons and synapses of a single integrated mind. The IGY proved how much could be accomplished by the human community when a unifying objective transcended political barriers. Yet all those unifying achievements were eclipsed by a single divisive event—in, of all places, space. Inspired by the IGY, both the United States and the Soviet Union had indicated they intended to launch earth-observing satellites. Typically, we reported our progress on a day-to-day basis; the Soviets, just as typically, offered only generalities that escaped public attention. The surprise launching of Sputnik 1, on October 4, 1957, jolted the United States like no other event since the Japanese attack on Pearl Harbor. In one blow, the Soviets shattered the world's perceptions of American technological and military superiority: the first man-made satellite was placed in orbit by a rocket that could be used as an intercontinental ballistic missile. America was made vulnerable as never before.

We recovered quickly, of course, and launched a crash program that restored and even increased American primacy. But the damage had been done. Sputnik completely diverted attention from the great unifying achievements and potential of the IGY.

Subsequently, President Dwight D. Eisenhower struggled to place space exploration on a more hopeful course. He told the American people: "The nations of the world face today another choice . . . that relates to the use of outer space. Let us this time, and in time, make the right choice . . ." Eisenhower's inspired choice was to create the National Aeronautics and Space Agency and to make sure that its charter included a commitment to international cooperation. In addition, Eisenhower ordered that a number of military space teams, including the Army's rocketry research unit headed by the legendary Wernher von Braun, be transferred to NASA's control. But, although NASA's statute kept it free and open, space activities remained a captive of the cold war as we battled the Soviets for primacy.

John F. Kennedy also struggled to liberate space exploration, but with no more success than Eisenhower. "Together let us explore the stars," he said in his inaugural address. A few days later, in his State of the Union address, Kennedy proposed initiating a program of U.S.–U.S.S.R. space cooperation in space science. "Both nations," he said, "would help themselves as well as other nations by removing these endeavors from the bitter and wasteful competition of the cold war."

A few weeks later, while the United States was suffering through the Bay of Pigs fiasco, the Soviets scored another triumph when Yuri Gagarin became the first human to orbit the earth. Desperate to restore America's image, Kennedy reversed himself and ordered his advisers to come up with a plan for a dramatic American "first" in space. The result was Kennedy's call—in May 1961—for a program that would place an American on the moon in a decade. The "moon race" was on.

During much of 1962 and 1963, U.S. space policy shifted almost from month to month. John Glenn's orbital flight buoyed Kennedy's spirits; he returned to his former call for cooperation; and talks were initiated between NASA and the Soviet Academy of Sciences. Subsequently, Soviet Premier Khrushchev told *Look* magazine that the Soviets might be interested in a joint moon expedition, and Kennedy brought it up at the June 1962 summit in Vienna. But Khrushchev tried to link it to Soviet disarmament demands, and Kennedy wisely backed off. Then, in 1963, the atmosphere warmed with the signing of the nuclear atmospheric test ban treaty. The Soviets again hinted they might be interested in cooperative activity in manned space flight. In response, Kennedy returned to his original inclinations: in a September speech before the United Nations, he called for a "joint expedition to the moon."

But by that time it was too late. NASA engineers, deep into plans and designs, worried about technical delays that might be caused by a shift to a joint effort. Congress even passed an amendment to NASA's appropriation, declaring that lunar-exploration funding could not be used for cooperative purposes without prior congressional approval, with the clear understanding that Congress wouldn't approve. Even though the moon project's cold-war motive had been superseded by events, and a joint expedition now seemed more in our interest, the project had acquired a momentum that Kennedy was unable to redirect.

It is a sad, sad story. Successive Presidents—a Republican (Eisenhower) and a Democrat (Kennedy)—saw the potential and the hope offered by East–West space cooperation. Again and again, they tried to respond to it. Again and again, they were dragged back into the quagmire of the cold war. Saddest of all was the overriding reason for their failure. It wasn't concern about technology transfer. Even military considerations played a secondary role. The driving force was succinctly summarized in a memorandum on space goals to John Kennedy from NASA administrator James Webb and Defense Secretary Robert McNamara. The issue, Webb and McNamara said, was "national prestige." Under the shallow inspiration of the cold war, the superpowers used the heavens as an arena to compete for applause on earth.

Perhaps fortunately, at least for the time, everyone but a few space specialists lost interest in the moon after we beat the Russians there. The great race was over. We had won. The audience went home.

Left to themselves, the competing space establishments began responding to their natural, healthier instincts. The first major step was taken by Dr. Thomas O. Paine, NASA's administrator at the time of the first moon landing. On Air Force One en route to the Pacific splashdown of the Apollo 11 astronauts, the first to walk

40

on the moon, Paine discussed the future of the space program with President Richard Nixon. Paine pointed out that the sheer size of future space ventures argued against an endless series of costly and duplicative races into space. Perhaps now, he said, we ought to look at the opportunities for cooperation. Nixon gave Paine the go-ahead to sound out key members of the Soviet Academy of Sciences.

It was, as usual, a slow and tedious process. But at least the volatile Khrushchev had left office. Gradually, discussions between the two countries assumed a businesslike tone. Three years of dedicated effort finally bore fruit on May 24, 1972, in Moscow, when Nixon and Soviet Premier Alexei Kosygin signed a five-year agreement on space cooperation.* It included a clause calling for "the docking of a United States Apollo-type spacecraft and a Soviet Soyuz-type spacecraft with visits of astronauts in each other's spacecraft," in 1975. The Apollo–Soyuz mission would be the first large-scale cooperative venture of the Space Age.

Apollo–Soyuz was basically a test of whether two very different systems could mesh on a complex space project without risk to the national security of either country. The test was successful. Neil Hutchinson, the U.S. flight director of Apollo–Soyuz, summed up what turned out to be its greatest frustration for those involved. "I wish there was another one of these flights. We've gone to all this trouble to learn how to work with these people . . . I could run another Apollo–Soyuz with a heck of a lot less fuss than it took to get this one going." Why wasn't Hutchinson given a chance? What a difference it would make today if Apollo–Soyuz had been followed by a steadily expanding program of cooperation that, as "Deke" Slayton pointed out, would give democracy the

---

* *Three other scientific exchange agreements were signed at the 1972 Moscow summit, dealing with health and medicine, environmental protection, and science and technology. Eventually, seven additional agreements were signed; they concerned transportation, atomic energy, housing, artificial heart research, energy, agriculture, and oceanography. Together, they became known as the "bilaterals."*

offensive on the space frontier. Why, if Apollo–Soyuz had worked so well, hadn't we at least tried to follow up?

But, of course, we had. A major follow-up program to Apollo–Soyuz was in fact initiated. At the time, few Americans realized its import and a golden opportunity was lost. Drawing on NASA's archives, I retraced the history of that ill-fated venture. The tale filled me with mounting wonder, regret, and sheer frustration.

The seeds were actually sown several years before Apollo–Soyuz, in 1969. That was the year President Nixon gave NASA administrator Tom Paine the green light to explore the opportunities for greater U.S.–U.S.S.R. cooperation in space. It was also the year Nixon decided that the successor to the Apollo moon program would be a space shuttle. In making that decision, Nixon rejected a broader (and costlier) proposal in which the shuttle would have served as a service vehicle for a space station. Instead, Nixon opted for an independent shuttle that would become operational in the 1980s.

Faced with a truncated shuttle mission and a mandate to explore cooperation with the Soviet Union and other nations, farsighted NASA planners reexamined the issue in Space Age terms. In the late summer of 1974, Dr. George M. Low, deputy administrator of NASA, received a technical memorandum from the Johnson Space Center in Houston, outlining "An International Space Activity." The memorandum noted that the United States was developing a "moderate lift logistic craft," the shuttle, that was meant to mate with a space station. Meanwhile, the Soviets already had a space station, Salyut, modular in design, that they were gradually upgrading to a multi-pod complex. Thus, U.S. and U.S.S.R. manned space-flight programs were proceeding along remarkably complementary lines: while we focused on a shuttle that was meant to service a space station, the Soviets focused on a space station meant to be serviced by a shuttle. The West Europeans were also keenly interested in manned space activities but had no plans for a sufficiently powerful launch vehicle.

The memorandum then entered into a technical discussion of the system elements of an international space station that would direct manned space exploration along a cooperative course while saving money over the long term. It would consist of a command center called a core module (or perhaps U.S. and Soviet semi-autonomous cores), plus a laboratory and service modules. Adjacent to them would be unmanned free-flight facilities for delicate scientific experiments where human presence would be intrusive. Sortie craft would service the unmanned facilities, and manned logistic craft (the U.S. shuttle and the Soviet Soyuz) would transport personnel and cargo.

NASA's internal initiatives received a major boost with the success of Apollo–Soyuz the following year. Now no one could say that the U.S. and the U.S.S.R. couldn't mount a complex joint mission. The groundwork had been laid.

In May 1977, after talks lasting several months, the U.S. and the U.S.S.R. signed an agreement on Cooperation in the Area of Manned Space Flight. It called for a Shuttle–Salyut Program and an International Space-Platform Program. Under the Shuttle–Salyut Program, our short-duration shuttle (only a maximum ten days in orbit) would be used to ferry scientific experiments to the long-duration Salyut station. Under the International Space-Platform Program, the two nations would define the objectives of an international station, consider possible designs, and formulate specific proposals for its implementation.

On November 14, 1977, just six months after the agreement was signed, an eighteen-member U.S. delegation arrived in Moscow to begin talks on the shuttle–Salyut program. The Americans were taken completely by surprise. They had expected a general discussion. The Soviets came in with specific proposals of solid scientific substance. Dr. Charles Kennell of UCLA, a member of the U.S. delegation, recalled the 1977 Moscow meeting in a letter in response to my written request: "The Soviets made it clear, both formally and in private remarks to me, that they were aware of

one of the principal American criticisms of the earlier Apollo–
Soyuz joint venture, namely, that it was largely a 'space spectacular'
with disappointingly little scientific return. The composition of
their delegation indicated, it seemed to me, that they wanted to
cure this impression. It contained three Academicians (Sagdeev,
Gasenko, and Shklovskiy) and other prominent scientists (Shulin,
Severniy, Kardashev, and Marov) whose work was also known to
me. The Soviets proposed in detail ambitious scientific projects in
eleven areas."

Later, another prominent member of the U.S. delegation, Dr.
Gerald Wasserburg of the California Institute of Technology, the
former chairman of COMPLEX, confirmed Kennell's impressions
in a private meeting in my office. Wasserburg, who had earned a
reputation as one of our toughest negotiators and who had abso-
lutely no illusions about the Russians, was nonetheless extremely
impressed by the caliber of their presentation. "Senator," he told
me, "the simple truth is that they were much better prepared than
we were."

The Soviet list of detailed experiments included X-ray astronomy, cosmic-ray research, materials processing, space biology and
medicine, space meteorology, radio astronomy, atmospheric research—all valuable and noncontroversial, mostly involving the
use of the Soviet space station in much the same manner that
scientists hoped to use the American space station to be built a
decade later. Merely for the experience it would provide in designing and orienting the American space station's mission, the
shuttle–Salyut program offered the United States enormous benefits.

When they broke up on November 17, 1977, the shuttle–Salyut
joint working groups agreed on a series of meetings in 1978—
March/April in Washington, July in Moscow, October in Washington—aimed at putting together a coordinated program for the
early 1980s.

The shuttle–Salyut joint working group never met again.

The international space-platform joint working group never even held its first meeting.

The United States pulled out of the entire program.

Why?

"I do not know precisely why," Kennell wrote me, "but I, for one, was disappointed that it did, because in my field of plasma physics the formal and informal interchanges between scientists in the U.S. and the U.S.S.R. had done much to develop our understanding of the subject, and had enhanced the U.S. programs." Kennell enclosed a copy of the shuttle–Salyut experiment recommendations prepared by a panel of scientists in his field who were assembled by NASA after the November meeting in Moscow. Their report was dated April 1978—just in time for the meeting that the United States canceled.

Why?

"Let's just say we didn't have a space policy," Gerald Wasserburg explained. "We didn't then and we don't now. The decisions on what we do in space are made episodically and too often with no reference whatsoever to space."

We turned our back on shuttle–Salyut and the international station in 1978 for essentially the same reason we launched a moon race and canceled the space cooperation agreement. We launched a moon race in reaction to the Bay of Pigs. We canceled the space agreement in reaction to Poland. We canceled shuttle–Salyut and the international station in reaction to Soviet policies in Africa and Soviet policies toward dissidents. The possibility that the activities we canceled might have been in the long-term interest of the United States as well as the cause of universal human rights—that the unique opportunities for democratic change offered by the Space Age could only be discovered and exploited by pursuing a forward-looking *long-term* policy—was never seriously considered. Our business was to react today without thought to tomorrow.

The shuttle–Salyut program and the international space-platform program were conceived by visionaries with their feet on the ground. In the best American spirit, they wanted to try something *new*, exciting, challenging, that might initiate a whole new era. Theirs was a truly new idea. But instead of exploring it, America's senior policymakers turned away from it. They couldn't see its unique promise. They couldn't see the Space Age. They were trapped in the mad destructive logic of the cold war.

6 / MARS

Did America's first settlers huddle together on the Eastern sea-board, waiting to solve all their social and economic problems before beginning their Westward march? Or did the march itself serve as a liberating force for democracy and for economic and scientific innovation? Since American dynamism was so much a product of the Western frontier, and that frontier had now been conquered, might not a new goal on the next frontier in space perhaps even be necessary for the continued vitality of our nation? While musing over those questions, I came across a reference to a book published in 1953 by the great rocket pioneer Wernher von Braun, entitled *The Mars Project,* and I ordered a copy from the Library of Congress. Von Braun had directed the design of the Jupiter rocket that catapulted our first satellite into orbit in 1958 and the giant Saturn rocket that took the first crew to the moon. What, I wondered, did he have in mind for Mars?

The Mars Project was a revelation. It consisted of complex designs and mathematical tables programming a manned mission to Mars to be carried out by "a flotilla of ten space vessels manned by not less than seventy men." The flotilla would be assembled in near-earth orbit over a period of eight months. The round-trip journey to Mars would last nearly three years, including thirteen months on the red planet.

In 1956, von Braun published a revised version of *The Mars Project,* in association with the scientist and writer Willy Ley. In this edition, entitled *Exploration of Mars,* the flotilla was reduced to two Mars ships assembled in orbit by a fleet of "shuttle rocket ships," consisting of unmanned cargo vessels and their winged, reusable passenger vessels designed to land on runways after completing orbital tasks. The winged shuttles would ferry the space construction crews back and forth to earth during the seven months it would take to assemble the Mars ships in orbit. (Orbital assembly was required because a Mars-bound launch from Earth would require more fuel than a manageable rocket could hold. Only by launching from a gravity-free orbit, with the lowest possible fuel requirements, was a manned Mars mission possible.)

Besides demonstrating the technical feasibility of a manned Mars mission, von Braun's proposal prefigured the American manned space program into the 1990s. There, in the 1950s, was a description of the winged shuttle of the 1980s. (Von Braun even called it a shuttle, and I assume NASA appropriated the name.) In von Braun's account of on-orbit assembly were the seeds of the space station of the 1990s. Both had been put forward as components of a manned mission to Mars. We now had the shuttle and were on the way toward the space station. How had we wound up building the components while abandoning the mission?

Politics. Von Braun's aspirations for a Mars mission as the primary target of our space program were shared by NASA's planners from the beginning. But in the spring of 1961 John Kennedy needed something relatively quick and dramatic, so he sent NASA racing to the moon instead.

Nonetheless, even while the Apollo moon program was underway in the 1960s, NASA awarded more than sixty Mars mission design contracts to aerospace companies. After we finally got the moon race out of our system, NASA planners, led by von Braun, tried to restore the original goal. In 1969, von Braun proposed a mission that would depart on November 12, 1981, reach Mars on August 9, 1982, and return to Earth on August 14, 1983. His proposal was incorporated into the report of a space task group appointed by President Nixon to establish objectives in space after Apollo. They offered three options, led by von Braun's Mars mission with shuttle and space-station components. The second option postponed Mars until the late 1980s. Option 3 included only the space station and the shuttle. With Vietnam devouring the federal budget and the national will, Nixon rejected all three options and elected to go only with a shuttle. All the missions we subsequently dreamed up for the shuttle, and were now dreaming up for the space station, had thus come after the fact. The original idea was to use the shuttle and the space station to take us to Mars in the 1980s.

The damage to our space program caused by that 1969 decision is only now beginning to show. A shuttle that was meant to lead us to Mars is being wholly justified as a vehicle for "commercializing" near-earth orbit, mainly by launching and servicing satellites. But, because unmanned launch vehicles for commercial satellites are often cheaper, the fastest-growing and surest customer for the shuttle is turning out to be the Department of Defense, which has a different agenda and a much roomier budget. The odds are that the same will eventually apply for the space station. Many of the scientific experiments for which it is being touted (especially for industry) will turn out to be far more economic if conducted on cheap, unmanned, free-flying platforms already under design in the U.S. and Europe. Manned space station activity will be taken over mainly by weapons designers and testers, for whom cost isn't a factor in the endless struggle with the Soviet Union for national survival, on earth and now in heaven.

The whole thing is out of kilter. The extraordinary economies promised by shuttle and space station will never be realized until they are allowed to do what they're supposed to do. They were conceived and designed to support the fundamental overriding objective of the Space Age—interplanetary exploration and settlement carried out across a broad expanse of time and space. They are equivalents of the government-financed roads and canals that opened up the American continent in the nineteenth century, or the interstate highway system which transformed our economy in the 1950s and which is still federally financed. Eventually, our space infrastructure will be capable of fostering commercially competitive enterprises offering economic benefits beyond our dreams, but first we have to give it *space* and *time*.

To learn whether the Mars mission idea began with von Braun, I traced American rocketry back to its beginnings, and made another discovery. America's Mars program really began in a cherry tree in Worcester, Massachusetts, in 1899. Sitting in the upper branches of the tree was a seventeen-year-old young man named Robert Goddard. The cherry tree was his private hideaway where he went to think and dream and make plans for his future. On that day in 1899, by his own later account, Goddard had a vision. In his mind's eye, he saw the planet Mars, red and gleaming in the darkness of space. And then, four years before the Wright brothers flew their first airplane, young Goddard imagined a device that could transport him across forty million miles of emptiness to that haunting luminous sphere. Robert Goddard spent the rest of his life working to turn his vision into reality. The by-product he left behind was the world's first successful rocket ship. Robert Goddard was the father of modern rocketry. His goal was Mars.*

Goddard had been inspired, in part, by the findings of nineteenth-century astronomers, especially the Italian Giovanni Schiaparelli, who in 1877 identified what he called *canali* on Mars, and the American Percival Lowell, who deduced the remains of a

---

* See the stimulating essay "Via Cherry Tree, to Mars," in Carl Sagan's Broca's Brain.

Martian civilization. Indeed, it seems that Mars has exerted a peculiar fascination on the human mind ever since our most ancient ancestors contemplated the heavens. Because of its unusual reddish color, many ancient civilizations associated the planet Mars with the bloody god of war or with plagues and floods. Others saw in that redness the river of life coursing through their veins. Whatever the case, the allure of Mars was of such historic persistence, and generated so many significant by-products (including the rocket), that it would be a foolishly narrow conceit to reduce its attraction to determining whether or not life existed there. Goddard and von Braun responded to the pull of Mars by building the first rocket and conceiving the first space shuttle, as their pioneer forebears, also inspired by a distant goal, had designed and built railroads and highways and revolutionary new modes of transportation and production.

But what about the other national leader in rocketry and space exploration, the Soviet Union? Perhaps I shouldn't have been surprised to learn that the man ranked alongside Robert Goddard as a herald of space flight was a self-taught Russian scientist-engineer named Konstantin Tsiolkovsky. In 1883, when Goddard was barely a year old, Tsiolkovsky (then twenty-six) wrote a paper speculating on how mechanical propulsion might best be generated in a gravity-free environment. His deductions led him, before anyone else, to the basic principles of rocketry. By the turn of the century, he was publishing designs of rocket engines. He was joined in his research by a small band of scientists who established Russia as the center of theoretical studies for manned space flight.

But it wasn't until the tsarist regime was overthrown that Tsiolkovsky came into his own. The Soviet Union was the first nation formally to endorse the goal of manned space flight. Their credo was Tsiolkovsky's famous "Fourteen Points," which included development of a rocket plane, space suits, closed-cycle life-support systems, space stations, colonies on other planets—all fully articulated in 1930. And the goal was Mars. Tsiolkovsky's heir, Frederick Tsander, had as his motto, "Forward to Mars." His rallying cry was echoed by scientists, politicians, and the thousands of members of rocket clubs that sprouted throughout the Soviet Union. Only in Germany (under the inspiration of Hermann Oberth) and in the United States was there comparable interest in rocketry. But neither matched the Soviets in their range of interest and almost mystical enthusiasm for the long-term prospects of manned space exploration.

Sputnik might have shocked the world much sooner were it not for the repressive policies of Stalinist Russia. Stalin didn't trust his aeronautical engineers any more than he did anyone else. His best rocket designers wound up in the Gulag in the 1930s, and their subsequent experiments with prototypes were carried out in prison camps. The German invasion added destruction to the isolation and chaos. Even so, Russian rocketry recovered quickly after the war—enriched by captured German booty and personnel and spurred by the priority assigned to developing a response to a U.S. strategy of containment. We had ringed the Soviet Union with air bases for bombers equipped with nuclear weapons. With a shortage of allies, Russia's leaders were unable to threaten us in the same manner. So they turned to their rocket designers to find a means to deliver nuclear destruction directly from the U.S.S.R. Their all too successful answer was the intercontinental ballistic missile.

But Soviet space interest and activities were clearly far more than a cold-war phenomenon. With them, as with us, space exploration interests and activities dated back to the turn of the century. Although less spectacular in its successes than ours, the post–World War II Soviet space development and exploration program had shown greater persistence and consistency, especially in manned space flight.

In the late fall of 1983, I obtained a draft of a report to be published by the Office of Technology Assessment, a research arm of the Congress, entitled *Salyut: Soviet Steps Toward Permanent Human Presence in Space.* The report noted that the United States pretty much gave up on manned space flight in the period between the conclusion of Apollo in 1972 and the first shuttle launch in 1982, but the Soviets maintained an unbroken commitment. At least one of their Salyut space stations had been in orbit almost continuously since 1971. Wrote OTA: "In some respects, the activities of the two countries in [manned space flight] have resembled the race between the tortoise and the hare: while the Soviet effort has featured apparently steady, incremental progression along well-defined lines of development, the United States has typically played catch-up, using its strong technological capacity to produce space achievements of startling virtuosity . . . Still, the Soviets have shown considerable perseverance, and their predictions about even bigger space stations—capable of housing large collections rather than small crews—should be taken seriously."

While we invented justifications as we went along, the Soviets had made clear from the beginning that the aim of their space station and its complementary platforms and vehicles was interplanetary exploration and settlement. In 1961, shortly after he became the first man to orbit the earth, Soviet cosmonaut Yuri Gagarin announced that the ultimate objective of his mission was—in the spirit of Tsiolkovsky and Tsander—Mars. In 1970, cosmonaut Alexei Leonov, who would later command the Soviet portion of Apollo–Soyuz, announced that the Russians were aiming for Mars. Soviet political leaders invoked the goal of interplanetary flight with the same open persistence. "Indeed," the OTA report concluded, "the Salyut space station may provide the core element of a future base necessary to ensure success of future trips to Mars."

Mars. It was there at the beginning, in both space programs. The Russians clung to it. We turned away from it. In so doing, we more than lost sight of an objective. We also lost a Space Age frame of reference for our extraterrestrial activities. The pull shifted from space to Earth; from building an infrastructure leading into space to inventing justifications for various disconnected space activities only incidentally related to the character and opportunities of the Space Age. We lost sight of what it was all about.

A Mars objective provided the reorientation in perception necessary to gain entrance into the Space Age. Mars meant interplanetary exploration and settlement on a scale of time and space such as had never before been attempted. The spin-offs—servicing satellites, developing pharmaceuticals—would continue and others of far greater significance would follow. But the entire enterprise would be perceived in a new light. We would begin to understand the meaning of the Space Age—how vast it really was and how best to exploit the unique opportunities it offered.

I was reminded of a chapter in John Huizinga's classic *Waning of the Middle Ages,* which described the transition from the Middle Ages to the Renaissance. Huizinga cited a passage in the notebooks of Michelangelo criticizing Jacob van Eyck, one of the great painters of the Middle Ages. Van Eyck's genius was distinguished by an exquisite attention to detail, by the refinement of every square centimeter in his crowded canvases. His weakness, the great Michelangelo explained, lay in an inability to give liberating expression to a new idea. Van Eyck was the brilliant spokesman of a dying age, ensnared in a web of detail that constituted the "real world" of his time. Never would his genius discover the awe-inspiring simplicity revealed in Michelangelo's *Creation of Adam.*

One critic called all of Michelangelo's work the expression of "an idea, struggling to free itself from its prison." It was the Renaissance itself. He could feel its emerging power. His art gave it inspiring form. So with Mars in the mind of man in our time. Mars incarnates the mystery and grandeur of a dawning Space Age. Humanity might postpone that age at enormous expense and waste. We might destroy ourselves in a final holocaust before we discover its saving potential. But we will never impose our narrow and stagnant cold war on the limitless heavens.

54

7 / LEGISLATIVE MANEUVERINGS

What Americans needed (and need) was a goal that dramatized the great challenge of the frontier in space: a goal that captured its immensity and uniqueness. Our forebears had such a goal. It was to carry democratic civilization across a sprawling continent to the Pacific Ocean. They didn't attain their visionary goal in a single generation. They proceeded in stages—first sending out expeditions of exploration, then building roads and railroads through the wilderness, finally installing settlements. But always, at every stage, they looked toward that distant goal. It pulled them forward and inspired a visionary determination and ingenuity such as the world had never known.

Without a comparable purpose—a frontier at once distant, inspiring, and attainable—America will never begin to exploit the potential of space. Modest scientific exchanges in space science must be perceived as building blocks to a future of awesome significance. Then decisions on whether to interrupt the process might be examined in terms of America's real long-term interests.

* * *

In November 1983, I drafted a short newspaper article that proposed a series of cooperative space missions of gradually increasing complexity, pointing toward an international manned mission to Mars at the turn of the century. For dramatic effect, I contrasted this program with Star Wars, which was projected to develop during the same time frame. The article praised the President for seeking to mobilize America's innovative can-do spirit toward a noble and transcendent objective. But it suggested that the objective might best be attained by "a mighty undertaking in space *with* the Soviets rather than against them." I concluded: "By the end of the twenty-first century, unmanned international scientific missions could be sailing to all the planets in the solar system and to the moons of Jupiter and Saturn. Manned spaceship traffic could steadily flow to scientific outposts and mining facilities on several asteroids, the moon and Mars. Our children would look up to a fever of activity in space, moving toward the outer limits of the solar system, aiming for the stars. Compared to that inspiring prospect, a high-ground space weapons program looks like an anthill."

I had never tried anything quite like this before. Politicians are only supposed to paint rosy pictures at the conclusions of after-dinner speeches, when no one takes them seriously. So I had to move on two tracks—limiting the pictures to occasional glimpses that wouldn't damage my credibility in the "real world," while pursuing the legislative effort to renew the space cooperation agreement.

It took five months for my "building blocks to Mars" article to find a publisher. After being turned down by the editors of several major newspapers, it was published in April 1984 by *Newsday*, in Long Island, New York. Painting that new picture would be a slow process.

Meanwhile, on February 9, 1984, the resolution calling for renewal of the U.S.–U.S.S.R. space cooperation agreement was reintroduced as a Senate Joint Resolution. This time, Clai Pell and

I were joined by Charles McC. Mathias of Maryland, the third-ranking Republican on the Senate Foreign Relations Committee. The language of the joint resolution was identical to its predecessor, except for a broadening of the final resolved clause, to give greater flexibility to negotiators.

My floor statement accompanying the joint resolution's introduction emphasized how renewed cooperation would provide increased returns for American science and new options for foreign policy-makers and save large sums of money for American taxpayers. I also appended two documents—a State Department evaluation of past U.S.–U.S.S.R. space cooperation activities and a letter to me from Christopher Kraft, director of the Johnson Space Center when it coordinated the U.S. contribution to Apollo–Soyuz.

Chris Kraft knew Apollo–Soyuz down to the last detail. In his letter, he described the mission's organization and objectives, leading to a "mutually beneficial" outcome. He went on: "On the other hand, there has been a great deal of speculation and sometimes uninformed accusation that the U.S. gave away some of its technological know-how while receiving little in exchange from the U.S.S.R. It is very doubtful, at least to my knowledge, that the U.S.S.R. received any technology from us that was not readily available in some unclassified documentation. We did find (at least through the people we dealt with) that . . . their knowledge of free world management techniques was naïve to say the least. Therefore, one could conclude that the knowledge they gained might be some form of technology transfer. However, it was the opinion of most of us at the Johnson Space Center that although they may have understood how we manage, they would find it very difficult to apply in their country because of the extreme differences in industrial and government structure."

I couldn't help chuckling to myself when reading Chris Kraft's letter. The "extreme differences" in management techniques he cited were not only traceable to democratic procedures, as Deke Slayton had pointed out. They were also, as Kraft noted, expressions of the difference between capitalist free enterprise and communism. If passing on that kind of information was technology transfer, then we had better put guards outside the doors of all our business schools and our businesses, with signs reading: "This is a Free Enterprise. Top Secret."

The State Department report further documented the benefits of cooperation. The report appeared in a broad evaluation of U.S.–U.S.S.R. scientific exchanges during 1981 and 1982, prepared for the Senate Foreign Relations Committee in order to determine whether the U.S. gained as much from the Soviets as we gave. It showed how, despite a further drop in cooperative activity following Soviet outrages in Afghanistan, American space scientists still managed to fill in large gaps in U.S. programs by exploiting the Soviets.

The advantages to the United States were particularly striking for manned space flight. At a November 1981 meeting in Washington, Soviet physicians provided medical reports from a Salyut earth-orbiting mission of 185 days and a later 75-day mission. In exchange, American physicians offered data collected from experiments in weightlessness simulators on the ground in Houston. Also, Soviet biologists discussed their plans for a bio-satellite mission that would send two primates into orbit. In exchange, our biologists discussed how we might participate in their mission, since we had nothing comparable scheduled.

While our life scientists were collecting new information from the Soviets in Washington, U.S. and Soviet planetary scientists held a "highly successful" meeting in San Francisco. Data on separate U.S. and Soviet missions were exchanged. Each side delivered reports on the current status of research in lunar-sample analysis, the geology of Mars, cosmic-dust studies, and related areas. After examining possible future missions, the scientists agreed to meet again in 1982 to establish "several kinds of coordinated efforts which could enlarge the scope of current bilateral activities." That was the progress cited by Dr. Eugene Levy in his letter to me, which he said was leading toward an agreement for coordinated exploration of Venus. "That Venus meeting was to have taken place in the Soviet Union in May 1982," the State Department report said, "but was not held due to the non-renewal of the U.S.–U.S.S.R. space agreement."

In March–April 1982, in the last official activity before the agreement expired, a number of U.S. scientists visited the Soviet Union, to be on hand when the Soviets' Venera 13 and 14 spacecraft touched down on the surface of Venus and to share in the important information the Soviets obtained. "No comparable U.S. information flow to the Soviet Union was possible during 1982," the report stated, because we weren't doing anything.

The State Department concluded on technology transfer for 1981: "The overall value of the scientific and technical information exchanged during 1981 would appear to be approximately balanced. It should be noted, however, that certain data (particularly biomedical data related to long-duration manned spaceflight) is available only from the U.S.S.R." For 1982: "For the five months of 1982 in which the U.S.–U.S.S.R. exchange activities took place under Space Agreement auspices, the overall value of the scientific and technical information clearly favored the U.S."

The State Department assessment exploded the myth that space cooperation with the Soviets had to be a one-way street. During the final year and a half of the space agreement, transfer of information and technology had been either balanced (1981) or in our favor (1982). In a sense, Soviet space science had helped carry our program through the lean years of the post-Apollo letdown and the diversion of NASA funds to shuttle development. While the politicians played politics, the scientists quietly helped each other out.

Two weeks after the joint resolution's introduction, Senators Pell, Mathias, and I sent a letter to John Gibbons, director of the Office of Technology Assessment, an investigative arm of the Congress, requesting a report on the "scientific risks and benefits" of U.S.–U.S.S.R. space cooperation that included "specific examples." Those examples were especially important. Obtaining them would require the involvement of those who knew the most about the two space science programs yet who were rarely consulted by foreign policy-makers—the scientists. Their expert testimony would prove invaluable during Senate hearings on our legislation.

By mid-April, our effort was off the ground. The Senate joint resolution had picked up fourteen co-sponsors, compared to two the year before. In the House, Congressman Mel Levine of California had introduced a companion measure with eighty co-sponsors. Most important of all, the Senate Foreign Relations Committee had scheduled hearings for June 6.

To broaden the base of support in the Senate, I decided to introduce a separate resolution that highlighted the least controversial aspect of space cooperation—space rescue. When a freighter comes upon a life raft in the Pacific Ocean, the captain doesn't inquire about the political ideology of its helpless occupants. Why shouldn't the universal rules of the sea also apply to the great cosmic ocean of space? Could we call space exploration an advance of civilization if we denied explorers the possibility of aiding one another in distress? As it happened, the United States, along with Canada and France, was already engaged in a remarkably successful Space Age search-and-rescue program with the Soviets. The program used orbiting satellites to pinpoint aircraft that had crashed in remote regions, or ships in distress. It was called COSPAS / SARSAT—acronyms for the contributing systems. Because it had been negotiated prior to the spring of 1982 cancellation of the U.S.–U.S.S.R. cooperation agreement, and out of deference to the French and Canadian participants, we allowed COSPAS / SARSAT to get underway in June 1982. Thank heaven. On September 9, an aircraft carrying three passengers disappeared in a remote corner of British Columbia in Canada. Within hours, a Soviet COSPAS satellite pinpointed the downed crew, all of whom had suffered serious injuries, and they were rescued. Since then, more than two hundred lives had been saved—most of them Americans or Canadians aboard downed aircraft whose distress signals had been picked up by the polar-orbiting Soviet COSPAS. If the U.S. and the U.S.S.R. could manage a successful joint rescue program *from* space, why not do the same *in* space?

No matter how my space-rescue resolution was drafted, I knew that it would be limited in its appeal without Administration endorsement. So a draft was sent to NASA for comment. If they okayed it, or revised it in an acceptable manner, I would have the Administration's Good Housekeeping Seal of Approval for at least one aspect of space cooperation.

And a lot more. The ponderous and secretive Soviet bureaucracy regulated activities with other nations by means of rigidly formal overarching agreements. Before President Reagan could sell grain to the Soviets, he first had to have a generalized grain agreement. Similarly, the U.S.–U.S.S.R. space agreement would have to be renewed before a meaningful space-rescue program could be negotiated. Although I didn't advertise it, Administration endorsement of a space-rescue resolution would also amount to implicit endorsement of my broader measure calling for renewal of the space cooperation agreement.

Still with the upcoming Senate hearings in mind, I contacted the Office of Technology Assessment, or OTA, with an informal suggestion. It didn't seem likely that the report requested by Pell, Mathias, and me could be completed in time for the hearings on June 6. But wasn't one chapter supposed to contain the results of a special symposium to be attended by space scientists from around the nation? Might that symposium be convened before the hearings, so the Foreign Relations Committee could receive its findings— early May, for instance—perhaps May 7 or 8?

Those suggested dates, which OTA accepted, were inspired by

another meeting I had learned about, which was set for Washington at the same time. On May 8, a national security and arms-control committee of the National Academy of Sciences would meet with a counterpart group from the Soviet Academy of Sciences. The Soviet delegation to the May 8 meeting would be headed by Dr. Yevgeny P. Velikhov, vice chairman of the Soviet Academy. It would include Dr. Roald Sagdeev, director of the Institute for Cosmic Research, which oversaw most of the U.S.S.R.'s space science activities. With the OTA symposium now scheduled for the same date, the next step was to bring them all into the same room.

Following several rounds of Geneva-like negotiations, a splendid "unofficial" dinner was organized and held on the evening of May 7 at the Brookings Institution in Washington. Dr. John Steinbruner, director of Foreign Policy Studies at Brookings and a member of the National Academy of Sciences committee, made available a private dining room with a large circular table around which the participants gathered. Joining Steinbruner from the National Academy of Sciences committee were Dr. Charles Townes, Nobel Prize-winning physicist from the University of California at Berkeley, and General Lew Allen, former Air Force Chief of Staff and currently director of the Jet Propulsion Laboratory in Pasadena, California, NASA's lead operational agency for unmanned space exploration programs. From the Soviet Academy of Sciences came Vice-Chairman Velikhov, Dr. Sagdeev, and Dr. Nikolai Kokoshin, deputy director of the Institute for United States and Canadian Affairs in Moscow. The thirteen OTA symposium participants were represented by Dr. Bernard Burke of MIT, the symposium chairman; Dr. Thomas Donahue of the University of Michigan, who was also chairman of the National Academy's Space Science Board; Dr. Tobias Owen of the State University of New York at Stony Brook; and my good friend and mentor, David Morrison. Senators Pell and Mathias had previous engagements, but I was joined in representing the co-sponsors of the space cooperation resolution by Senator Jeff Bingaman of New Mexico.

I couldn't have asked for a better lineup. Of the Russians, Sagdeev was the most approachable, perhaps because he had spent so much time at international space conferences. He and the OTA symposium scientists greeted one another like old friends. Yet Sagdeev clearly deferred to Velikhov, seated on my right, a stocky, clear-eyed physicist who spoke quietly, deliberately, with accustomed authority. Dr. Townes is what I like to call one of nature's aristocrats. Relaxed and outgoing, he made his mark early at MIT and went on to serve Presidents and cabinet secretaries; he knew everyone, including Velikhov, who greeted him as an equal. General Allen is a tall, angular man of natural reticence, obviously more used to receiving information than to delivering it; he listens intently and responds with great intelligence and a minimum of words.

After starting off the discussion, I spent most of my time observing and taking mental notes. I couldn't help comparing this dinner with a public luncheon for Velikhov which I had attended earlier in the day. There the topic was arms control and the air was rich with ideological rhetoric and posturing. But this dinner was different. Here, in privacy and among peers, the dinner guests were like shrewd businessmen testing the market for each other's products.

Velikhov opened cautiously. He volunteered proposals for joint earthquake prediction and studies of the magnetosphere. Later, with a nod from Velikhov, Sagdeev mentioned Venus. The Venus suggestion set off a spirited discussion that grew more and more detailed, until it almost seemed as if the group was on the verge of writing up an agreement.

I concluded one of the most educational evenings I had ever spent by inviting each participant to make a summary statement. Without exception, they proposed greater cooperation. But it had to be businesslike, without political posturing. I got the feeling that none of them took much pleasure in seeing space played up as a three-ring circus where nations performed for the sake of prestige. Space was for them an immense challenge that demanded well-reasoned policies and down-to-earth planning and engineer-ing. In a word, it was *big*. Until policy-makers realized how big it really was, we wouldn't get very far.

On the way out, chatting with Dave Morrison, I mentioned my surprise at the detail of the discussions, considering the Soviets' well-known penchant for not revealing their plans. "We discovered that they had often held back in the past because they were em-barrassed at what they had to offer," Dave explained. "But they have now been running interplanetary missions for almost two decades, and with each launch they grow more confident. The international Halley's comet project, where they are sending the first two probes, followed by the Europeans, then the Japanese, with the U.S. contributing our ground-based tracking network—that's been a real breakthrough for them. They are truly a part of the international community now, with their own special contri-butions to offer. And that has made them more open."

I was unable to attend the OTA symposium the following day, but that evening I read a staff memo on the outcome. The thirteen participating scientists represented as many different institutions from around the nation. They were selected for their comple-mentary stature in the major fields of space research, such as astrophysics, planetary science, solar-terrestrial physics, and the life sciences. In each area, they found considerable opportunity for mutually beneficial U.S.–U.S.S.R. cooperation. One especially in-teresting (and easy) proposal in astrophysics involved mounting Spacelab experiments in the Soviet Salyut to take advantage of the greater duration of manned Salyut flights (upwards of two hundred days, compared to seven to ten days for Spacelab aboard our shuttle). Life scientists at the symposium also made several additional sug-gestions for taking advantage of Salyut for experiments in long-duration flight which would be useful in preparing for our own space station. Four years after we canceled it, the shuttle–Salyut program seemed more in our interest than ever. Another sugges-tion, in planetary science, called for coordinating planning for already scheduled unmanned scientific missions to Mars by the

U.S.S.R. in 1988 and the U.S. in 1990—a significant opportunity on the road to manned exploration of Mars.

In late May, as the OTA panelists were exchanging final drafts of their report for presentation at the June 6 Foreign Relations Committee hearing, that event was abruptly canceled—in effect, by the KGB. On May 2, Andrei Sakharov started a hunger strike to protest the Soviet government's refusal to permit his wife, Yelena Bonner, to travel abroad to receive medical treatment for a heart ailment. Twice before, in 1975 and 1981, this courageous man had employed the same device to gain humane treatment for himself and his wife. But this time the twice-humiliated KGB moved in swiftly and cut off all contact between the Sakharovs and the West. As the protests increased, so did the demands for action. But what should be done? Inevitably, cries arose for sanctions and for signs of solidarity by Sakharov's fellow scientists in the West.

I felt caught in the middle. There could be no excuse for Soviet behavior in this instance, as in so many others. But what was the best response? We couldn't possibly pursue a meaningful long-term policy that pushed for greater Soviet openness when all the KGB had to do to block our efforts was create an incident. We were prisoners of a process of action and reaction that virtually guaranteed the perpetuation of all that we deplored. By the end of May, the political climate was simply too hot to discuss U.S.–U.S.S.R. cooperation of any kind. The June 6 Senate hearing was called off. Isolation, mistrust, suspicion, and oppressiveness had won another round.

At no time did I equate our moral position with that of the Soviets. But being the good half of a closed loop of insanity wasn't good enough. We simply had to find a way to transcend this madness.

In mid-June, I finally received a reply from NASA on my space-rescue resolution. After considering the draft for two months, they had responded with a version acceptable to the Administration.

Their draft emphasized international treaty commitments defining astronauts as "envoys of mankind" and providing for search-and-rescue cooperation when astronauts landed on the soil of a foreign nation. At the same time, they had accepted the basic thrust of my draft, including a significant reference to future space-station cooperation. It looked fine. I quickly gained support from Senate Republicans and was working on a floor statement, when President Reagan beat me to it.

On June 27, the President delivered a speech to a Washington conference on U.S.–Soviet exchanges in which he listed a number of cooperative activities being proposed to the Soviets, including a "joint simulated space-rescue mission in which astronauts and cosmonauts would carry out a combined exercise in space to develop techniques to rescue people from malfunctions in space vehicles." A space-rescue mission! I knew that prior to such speeches the White House canvassed agencies for suggestions of specific proposals. In this case, the White House request had reached NASA while my space-rescue resolution was under review. Perhaps it had contributed to the inspiration, along with a proposal from James Oberg, the Soviet space specialist, who had earlier suggested a shuttle–Salyut rendezvous to test out rescue procedures.

I was also pleased that the President had endorsed the principle of cooperation. In his speech he said: "Civilized people everywhere have a stake in keeping contacts, communication and creativity as broad, deep and free as possible. The Soviet insistence on sealing their people off and filtering and controlling contact and the flow of information remains the central problem." Agreed. I hoped that the June 27 speech meant that our open society would be more creative about using our openness as an instrument of policy.

The next day, with a bow to the President, I introduced the space-rescue resolution. It was referred to the Senate Foreign Relations Committee, whose chairman, Charles Percy, quickly asked to be added as a co-sponsor. He also advised me that the canceled hearing on the space cooperation resolution would be rescheduled for mid-September. The double-resolution gambit had paid off well.

Due to the Presidential election campaign, Congress would probably recess in late September or early October. That didn't leave much time to move the measure out of committee and to the Senate floor for action. It was a long shot, maybe a hundred to one for a resolution of this sort. I felt pleased. The odds were improving.

8 / BEYOND
THE OPPOSITES

No aspect of space cooperation caused me greater personal anguish than the issue of human rights. It wasn't only the Sakharovs. Behind them stood countless others imprisoned for the crime of believing in freedom. How could I suggest cooperation with a regime opposed to my fundamental values? And yet, even as that question disturbed me profoundly, another attitude asserted itself. It belonged to a tradition inherited from the Orient and it existed alongside the Western values and religion I had adopted. I saw no contradiction in those two traditions from two sides of the world—only a mutual strengthening.

The Eastern tradition was passed through my father, Kingoro Matsunaga, who was my greatest early influence. At the age of nineteen, Kingoro ran away to America from a monastery school in Japan where his father had sent him to study for the priesthood in the Shinto faith. His motives were probably no different from those of many millions of American immigrants who sought a new life in the great land of opportunity.

Kingoro settled in Hawaii, on the island of Kauai, where he

worked on a sugar plantation as a field hand and a reservoir tender. There he met and married my mother, also a Japanese immigrant. Unable to support his family of seven children on a field worker's wages, he left the sugar plantation to work as a stevedore. This was at a time when cargo ships were anchored out in deep water offshore and loaded from little vessels towed by motorboats. One day, as my father was loading sugar in the hold of a ship swaying in rough water at Port Allen, Kauai, an avalanche of hundred-pound sugar bags came crashing down on him, burying him completely. He was rushed to a nearby hospital and the doctors offered little hope. In his hospital bed, barely able to speak, fifty-five-year-old Kingoro Matsunaga made a personal vow, with his grieving wife and seven children as witnesses. If God would save his life, he said, he would dedicate the remainder of his years to spiritual pursuits. My father survived and he kept his vow. After he came home, at his request my brothers and I built a Shinto temple for him in the back yard of our home.

Instead of retreating into the past, as we feared he might, my father brought the past into the present. He became a lay minister intent on applying his faith and learning to contemporary problems. In his own limited way, he studied incessantly—history, art, literature, politics, and theology.

Above all, he pursued the reconciliation of the philosophies of East and West. In his belief in the creative powers of the individual and the power of righteousness, my father showed his commitment to Western principles that he had traveled across an ocean to embrace. In his belief in the harmony of all living things, in the essential unity of opposing forces, he drew on Eastern philosophy. When I left my native Kauai in 1937 for the University of Hawaii in Honolulu, my father agreed to my living in the home of Reverend Takie Okamura, the first Christian missionary sent from Japan to the United States. He told me that he hoped I would learn from the religions of both the West and the East, and above all seek to reconcile them, so that both traditions might be enriched.

I have always tried to follow my father's ecumenical precepts. I found them especially valuable for addressing one of the most important public issues of our time—moral equivalence. Essentially, moral equivalence is a product of frustrations felt by certain Americans with the policies of their government. That frustration with American policies leads to a dangerously romanticized view of the policies of America's adversaries. During the depression of the 1930s, some Americans romanticized Stalinist Russia. Later, during the Vietnam era, many critics of the policies of the Johnson and Nixon Administrations romanticized the oppressive government of North Vietnam.

My father's conception of opposing forces rejected moral equivalence. He viewed Judeo-Christian morality, with its pronounced distinction between good and evil, as a major contribution to civilization as a whole. It was a powerful force for the activation of human conscience and thus for human decency and compassion. To that great Western moral tradition, Kingoro offered an Eastern complement. "If this concept can be integrated into Western morality, and vice versa," he told me, "we will have the best of both worlds." That complementary Eastern concept he called "beyond the opposites" and he related it to a very Eastern idea of *dynamic* equivalence.

If moral equivalence is a trap, so is the dynamic equivalence that develops when the party that is right in a conflict falls too much under the influence of the party that is wrong. Good will always be right, evil will always be wrong, yet the dynamic equivalence of a persistent action-reaction cycle will severely restrict good in its struggle with evil. Instead of being creative, it will succumb to compulsive reaction. Instead of being itself, it will depend more and more on the behavior of its opposite for a sense of identity and purpose.

U.S.–U.S.S.R. relations offer an example of the dangers of dynamic equivalence. Our policies consist too much of episodic reactions to their episodic actions. Absent is a clear-cut positive policy that reaches beyond the action-reaction cycle onto a plane where democracy's unique strengths might be consistently applied. With those thoughts running through my mind, I set to work composing an article that eventually appeared in *The Washington Post* on September 9, 1984, the Sunday before the Senate hearing on the space cooperation resolution:

> The case of Andrei Sakharov and Yelena Bonner dramatizes the central question of our nuclear age:
>
> How are two nations which hold the fate of the world in their hands to relate to one another when their ruling value systems stand at diametrically opposing poles?
>
> During the past fifteen years, two sharply contrasting U.S. policies have emerged. The Nixon–Ford–Kissinger Administration practiced what Richard Nixon aptly called "hardheaded detente." Its tools were trade and other forms of cooperation, combined with discreet pressure applied as part of a process of continuing negotiation.
>
> Although it produced considerable flexibility for lateral movement, "hardheaded detente" could not last as an American policy for the same reason it held so much appeal to the Soviet leadership: it lacked moral content. Its goal was world order in the classic European sense. It was suspicious of internal forces for change that threatened established ruling elites—in the Soviet Union, Chile, wherever.
>
> Jimmy Carter remedied that defect with a vengeance. He placed human rights at the center of his policy toward the Soviet Union and repeatedly "punished" (a word he favored) the Soviets for morally unacceptable behavior. The tools employed by Carter to administer punishment were, to a considerable extent, the various components of the web of interdependencies developed by Nixon–Ford–Kissinger.
>
> Under Ronald Reagan, that moralistic emphasis reached an apex with the description of the Soviet Union as the "focus of evil," as relations between the superpowers deteriorated and the arms race accelerated.

71

Which approach is preferable? Each, in my view, contains serious deficiencies. A policy in tune with American values and interests requires both moral concern and tactical flexibility, both calculation and compassion.

One way to serve American values and interests at once would be to establish cooperative activity as an overriding national objective to be pursued with calculated sophistication and moral determination. This policy would replace the prevailing vacillation between no contacts and an uncritical pursuit of contacts, which the Soviets exploit by limiting their participation to party hacks. It would set strict standards for cooperation and push them hard.

A policy of aggressive cooperation would recognize that the chief enemy is less world communist ideology, which takes many evolving forms (China, Hungary, Yugoslavia), than it is the repressive Soviet police state, which is compulsively hostile to any evolution at all, communist or otherwise.

Instead of responding to repugnant Soviet behavior by cutting off contacts as "punishment" (which actually makes work easier for the police state apparatus), we would keep up the pressure, constantly pushing for new and expanded contacts of substance in the teeth of Soviet repression. Our principal target would be the emerging scientific and technical elite, the most sophisticated and cosmopolitan segment of Soviet society, who enjoy the highest status, upon whom the totalitarian power structure depends for running the system.

In pursuing that target, we could expect much more support than now from our European and Japanese allies, who already favor increased cooperation and greater flexibility in dealing with the Soviets.

Would such a policy legitimize Soviet policies of repression toward Sakharov, Bonner, and others? On the contrary, it would constitute the strongest and most effective rejection of those policies. The Soviet police apparatus thrives on isolation. Why assist its efforts? Under present conditions, whenever they want to tighten the screws at home, they need only create an incident. We have handed them flexibility at our expense. In an important sense, American policy has made itself hostage to the KGB.

A policy of aggressive cooperation might best be launched with a proposal to do something big with the Soviets. It must be a long-term undertaking that locks them into an expanding program of joint activity. Soviet policy-makers must find it sufficiently appealing to stay in, although it places their reactionary system of internal controls increasingly at risk.

One promising possibility is an international manned mission to Mars in the twenty-first century. It could be put forward as an alternative to competing Star Wars space weapons systems, which would otherwise be developed in the same time frame.

Unlike Star Wars, it requires no technology breakthroughs and thus would be far less costly. Unlike Star Wars, which would polarize scientific inquiry on the greater frontier of space, it would mobilize the world's best scientists and engineers in a common endeavor on behalf of all humanity. Unlike Star Wars, it would mandate ever greater openness across an expanding front, to the thriving benefit of democratic values and interests. And unlike Star Wars, our allies would welcome it with relief and excitement, for it would be a response to the greatest problem of our time that is wholly in tune with the best in the American character.

Joint activity on a grand scale would respond to the deepest aspirations of Andrei Sakharov. In the late 1960s and early 1970s, Sakharov sought to nudge the Soviet Union in precisely that direction. Then the police apparatus moved in and reestablished the us-versus-them condition upon which it thrives.

"Any action increasing the division of mankind, any preaching of the incompatibility of world ideologies and nations is madness and a crime," Sakharov wrote. With such utterances, his descent from official favor began, until, alone and isolated, he could retain his integrity only by lashing back at his captors.

But we should not confuse his entrapped response with the deep universal spirit that moved him to seek the intellectual freedom which must inevitably ensue from expanded communication and joint activity on an international scale. We have it in our power to resurrect that noble spirit. All we need is the will and determination—and the leadership.

Although I didn't expect all human-rights activists to agree, I hoped that they would at least recognize that the proposed policy of sustained "aggressive" cooperation was aimed at using our values as weapons in the struggle and taking the offensive for a change.

But we would have to stay clear of the KGB trap. To the extent it succeeds, a policy of sustained cooperation will create anxieties that trigger outrageous clampdowns. At those moments, it is imperative that we *not* react by breaking off contact but instead push publicly even harder for expanded contacts along a gradually expanding front.

The victory democracy needs, which would produce the greatest triumph for human rights, is a victory of the sort my father aspired to—a universal victory that carries us beyond the opposites and liberates our ideals.

THREE

UNEXPECTED POSSIBILITIES

9 / A SPACE AGE MISSION FOR THE U.S. AIR FORCE

On May 25, 1984, the American Astronautical Society invited me to speak to the Third Annual Military Space Symposium in Washington. I was part of a congressional panel on "Pro and Con on Military Use of Space" which included Senator Malcolm Wallop and Congressmen George Brown and William Carney. Since Wallop and Carney were outspoken advocates of an accelerated space-weapons program, I assumed they were the "pros" and Brown and I the "cons."

By then, I was becoming accustomed to the unexpected whenever a Space Age perspective was applied to a familiar issue. Working on the military space speech proved to be no exception. I felt comfortable with neither pro nor con. In this case, my own military experiences played a role, too.

Upon graduation from college in June 1941, I accepted a commission as a second lieutenant in the U.S. Army, and immediately volunteered for active duty. War loomed on the horizon and I was proud to be in uniform, prepared to defend our threatened nation. Six months later the Japanese attacked Pearl Harbor. An invasion of Hawaii seemed imminent. During the immediate crisis, no one questioned my loyalty or that of the 1,565 Japanese-American soldiers serving in Hawaii. But soon after the Japanese Navy was decimated in the battle of Midway and the danger of an invasion receded, we were stripped of our arms and shipped to Camp McCoy, Wisconsin, where we were held like prisoners of war. The only reason: although we were American citizens, our facial appearance resembled that of the enemy. In a petition signed by every member of our exiled unit, we pleaded with President Franklin D. Roosevelt to grant us the right to prove our loyalty in combat against the enemy. When our prayers were finally answered, the demonstration of rejoicing among grownup men is something I shall never forget. Our arms were returned to us and as the 100th Infantry Battalion (Separate) we were sent to army camps in Mississippi and Louisiana for combat training, then onto troopships headed across the Atlantic.

We landed at Salerno, Italy, on September 26, 1943, with units of the 34th Red Bull Division—young men from Iowa, Minnesota, Nebraska, and the Dakotas. Our mission was to advance up the boot of Italy, and we never stopped. Together with other Japanese-Americans who volunteered to form the 442nd Regimental Combat Team, we became known as the Go for Broke regimental combat team, the most highly decorated unit in the entire military history of the United States, with nine Presidential United Citations.

Many times, as our unit fought its way northward, I came face to face with the conflicting impulses of war. They animated me, rejuvenated me, saved, saddened, and sickened me. Never had I felt so intimately bound to those around me, never so quick, so alert, yet so blindly intoxicated and brutalized. Early one morning, after having seen many of my comrades killed and wounded, as I myself lay wounded beside a stone wall on Hill 600, at the foot of Monte Cassino, I wrote a poem in the notebook I carried in my knapsack.

When in the light of thought I ask
  Myself; Just who am I and what,
What lasting imprints good or ill,
  Have I for future mortals wrought?
'Tis then my pride in vainness cries,
  My ego ebbs to naught from high,
And sadly do I realize
  The plight of many a soul as I;
Be born to live, to suffer, die,
  Unseen, unheard, unknown, unknelled;
Like chips upon a checkerboard
  No choice, no will, resigned, compelled.

Let patriots wave and sing and shout,
  Let politicians treaties seal;
Our souls which rise from wounded, maimed,
  Are dead to things untrue, unreal.

The words mattered far less to me—I was twenty-three—than the feelings they awakened. My heart was numb. The caring cadences of poetry restored it to life. In the act of capturing hopelessness and madness, poetry awakened feelings of hope and sanity and made me feel human again. I turned to it frequently in combat, as I would later at a military hospital in Naples, where I wrote whimsical poems to the nurses who tended me and the doctors who cut into my flesh to remove pieces of a German land mine.

No longer fit for combat duty, I was reassigned to the replacement depot command—first in Naples, then in Oran, Algeria. My job was to prepare officer replacements for combat. I composed a lecture for platoon leaders—second lieutenants, and first lieutenants like myself—on the most important requirement for success in combat: the will to fight. "It is my belief that the greatest contribution you as an officer and a leader can make toward shortening this war is to spread among yourselves and among your men that will to fight," I wrote. I described the need for platoon leaders to set an example by their "will to fight" and explained how the 100th Battalion's commitment to combat had made it "the fightingest unit on the Italian front."

Did those lectures on the will to fight make me a warmonger? Did those poems on the awfulness of war make me a peacenik? Could a soldier be both?

Yes, and more. My military experiences left me with an abhorrence of war and a deep respect and affection for the military. Armies rarely start wars. They are called into action in response to the demands of the nation they serve. More than a century ago, a French poet and soldier wrote, correctly I think, that an army is treated "according to a nation's needs, either with contempt or exaggerated honor." Buffeted by shifting tides of opinion, professional soldiers find an anchor in their commitment to one another and to the performance of duty with honor and skill. The Army, I learned, is a kind of super-charged community whose ideals derive from earthy bonds of brotherhood and loyalty to the nation the Army serves.

Later I read a great deal in military history in order to better understand the origins and evolution of the military. Although their assigned mission was war, their inherited structure and virtues suggested a broader function. Mobility, cohesion, discipline, leadership under life-threatening conditions, the ability to operate efficiently in remote regions—although uniquely united in the military, those qualities were not uniquely associated with the conduct of war. Perhaps, I thought, armies had evolved in response to additional challenges.

Nowhere, I learned, was that more true than in the United States. Men like Washington and Jefferson were opposed to large standing armies on principle. But, looking to the examples of ancient Rome and contemporary France, America's Founding Fathers were equally drawn to the potential of the military as a civilizing, nation-building instrument on the frontier. America's first and still most glorious expedition of exploration was led by two Army officers—Lewis and Clark. They set a pattern for military-led scientific expeditions that endured well into the twentieth century. America's first college to offer a degree in engineering was the United States Military Academy at West Point. For nearly half a century of national expansion, West Point served as the nation's primary training center for engineers, while its instructors helped set up the first engineering schools at other universities.

During our century-long period of continental expansion, civil engineering, scientific expeditions, and the U.S. Army were one in the public mind. The elite Army Corps of Topographical Engineers mapped the entire continent and built roads and railroads from one end to the other. And wherever they went, they brought scientists—zoologists, botanists, geologists, geographers, paleontologists, illustrators, hydrologists. The Army not only mapped the continent and opened it to transportation and settlement; they also catalogued it. The unparalleled natural-history collection of the Smithsonian Institution was derived largely from Army-led expeditions. The thirteen-volume *Pacific Railroad Reports* of the Topographical Engineers ranks as one of the most extraordinary scientific compilations of all time.

Perhaps the most fascinating chapter in the Army's curiously unknown history concerns our national parks. The Army literally saved them. Yellowstone was established as the first National Park in 1872, under the Interior Department. But Interior lacked the means to police it or the will to resist local speculators, squatters, and poachers. Yellowstone was on the way to disappearing when an Army detachment was brought in and its commander named park superintendent. A complete transformation took place. Army troops arrested poachers and squatters; they stocked mountain streams with fish, enforced rules against defacement and littering, planted millions of trees, and protected Yellowstone's virgin forests from illegal cutting.

When the all-powerful railroad lobby in Washington pushed

for a railroad through Yellowstone, the park superintendent, an Army engineer, wrote Congress that Yellowstone's "purity and quiet [would be] destroyed and broken by the noise and smoke of the locomotive." For twenty years, the Army fought bill after bill until the railroad lobby finally surrendered. As the Army had earlier promoted railroads, so it now fought them—in both cases, at the nation's behest and with honor and incorruptibility.

So successful was the Army in Yellowstone that troopers were called in to rescue Yosemite, Sequoia, and General Grant parks as well. Along the way, the Army established a governing framework for our national parks that served as the model for the National Park Service, state and local park units, and other park systems throughout the world. In fact, the first U.S. Park Rangers were soldiers who exercised the option given them to remain in the parks when the Army pulled out early in this century.

"Blessings on Uncle Sam's soldiers," wrote John Muir. "They have done their job well and every pine tree is waving its arms with joy." Muir, of course, was America's foremost naturalist— the founder of the Sierra Club.

Other unrecognized Army success stories include worldwide disaster-relief activities, for which mobile military units are perfectly suited, and even the rescue and successful management of the Civilian Conservation Corps—another tale no one seems to remember. Franklin Roosevelt proposed the CCC in his first Inaugural Address in March 1933. A deadline of July 1 was set for building and equipping 1,300 camps for 250,000 CCC workers. By May, only fifty camps had been built, and the CCC was on the verge of collapse. At that point, FDR called in the War Department. Within sixty days, the Army assembled and housed the largest peacetime government labor force in history. To make sure it stayed in business, a Reserve Army officer was detailed to manage each CCC camp for the duration. As the Army had saved our national parks, it also saved the CCC.

There is a similar and typically forgotten story for the U.S. Navy. Navy officers led expeditions of exploration and inquiry to every watery corner of the globe—Rodgers and Ringgold in the North Pacific, Wilkes in Antarctica and the South Seas, Perry in Japan, Peary to the epic discovery of the North Pole, Byrd in the Antarctic, Lynch to the Dead Sea, Herndon and Gibbons up the Amazon. The first program of worldwide weather observations was organized in 1858 at the suggestion of U.S. Navy Commander Matthew Fontaine Maury, founding director of the United States Naval Observatory. Under that program, warships of all nations adopted standard forms to record weather and oceanic phenomena and agreed to pool their information, even in time of war. Maury wrote:

> Rarely before has there been such a sublime spectacle presented to the scientific world: all nations agreeing to unite and cooperate in carrying out one system of philosophical research with regard to the sea. Though they may be enemies in all else, here they are to be friends.

Commander Maury later proposed a nationwide weather service. He was ahead of his time. Not until 1870 was such a service established by (who else) the Army Signal Service, forerunner of the U.S. Weather Bureau.

When did those extraordinary activities cease? How did we forget them? Looking back over our nation's history, it's easy to detect the cutoff point. Our perspective of the military mission—our *memory* of it—altered radically with the coming of the cold war and the nuclear age. In the span of a generation, we created the largest peacetime military establishment in our history and gave it the narrowest mission ever conceived. Before, the mission of the warrior was either combat or exploration and discovery. Now the mission had been reduced to military preparedness as an end in itself.

Preparedness for what? For the annihilation of the world? It's easy enough to say that the military must prepare for a war that must never be fought. But that still leaves our uniformed services with no outlet for their restless energies but the endless refinement of their arsenal of weapons. Like so many other institutions, the military has been made prisoner of a logic that perpetuates a madness. At one time, the sacred center of the military institution was "operations"—action. Now it's "procurement"—consumption. The military consumes more and more, while, aside from playing war games, it has less and less that is meaningful to *do* in the sphere of *action*. As thermonuclear weapons make all-out war unthinkable, the cold war seduces the military with an orgy of high-tech consumption and steals its heart and soul.

No branch of the military services has suffered more than the Air Force. The U.S. Air Force came into being shortly after the end of World War II, just as we entered the cold war and just as a new frontier opened up in space. I tried to imagine the mission of the youngest service under other circumstances. In the nineteenth century, the Army had allied with science in opening the Western frontier. Our Navy had led scientific expeditions to the ocean frontiers. Without the cold war, the Air Force, the most scientifically oriented of the services, would surely have charted the great new frontier in space.

But, instead, President Eisenhower created NASA. Budding Air Force space programs came under NASA's control. Eisenhower really had no choice. Faced with the cold war's nightmare vision of a permanently polarized world living under the threat of total annihilation, we polarized our perceptions of military and civilian activity. The military became guardians of the nuclear nightmare, and its activities were separated from society. We created new "peaceful" agencies to take up responsibilities that had been a part of our military's richly textured and now forgotten history. That split in memory and perception, in turn, helped insure the cold war's permanence.

In the bleak context of the cold war, the creation of NASA guaranteed the militarization of space and the eventual subversion of NASA. For it touched off a space race in our own country between the civilian and military communities. The winner would be the one whose mission had the highest priority. NASA postponed the inevitable by gaining support for the Apollo moon program *as a contest with the Soviets.* But when that race ended and no other polarizing "threat" appeared, NASA's brief golden age ended. As NASA's budget declined, the military's space budget increased. In the 1980s, DOD took over the lead in space funding.

With the ascendancy of military confrontation in space, the military significance of *all* space science and technology inevitably expanded, thus adding fuel to the process. For with space confrontation came secrecy and narrow self-absorption. If events continue along their present course, the shuttle and the space station will mark not the beginning of an era of expanding hope and expectation but its end.

The chief beneficiary of NASA's decline would appear to be the Air Force, especially since Star Wars activities have been consolidated under its command. But, for the Space Age, that evolution is as disastrous for the Air Force as it is for NASA. The Air Force manages ICBMs buried in silos scattered over the Great Plains. It manages the North American Air Defense Command buried in a Colorado mountainside. Soon it will manage a remote-controlled space-weapons system from a space operations center buried in another Colorado mountain. The U.S. Air Force is going underground—literally—without seeming to recognize the supreme irony of it all.

The men and women of the Air Force—whose mission is to *fly*—have been completely and utterly conned. The Strategic Defense Initiative provides an inspirational challenge only for the procurers and designers of weapons. Even when operational, it will bring Air Force personnel as close to space as a group of teenagers entombed in a steel-and-granite video-game amusement arcade.* The true challenge of space, as of other earthbound frontiers, lies in the daring discovery and exploration of distant new worlds.

The Air Force is meant to meet the challenge of space exploration, not divert us from it. Space-weapons systems will breed horizontally. They will spin off countless sub-systems in the same earth-locked orbit. What we really want won't matter, any more than it does now. Each year the ever-expanding "requirements" of the cold war will make the decisions for us.

From a Space Age perspective, the only saving solution, for all concerned, is a space exploration policy that aligns the Air Force with NASA. NASA would handle conception and design of all space missions, and the operation of unmanned missions. To the Air Force would fall operational direction of manned space exploration that would be carried out openly and in cooperation with other spacefaring nations. Air Force pilots, crews, and ground support teams would be in charge of transporting scientists and (eventually) settlers to distant spheres. The mission of the U.S. Air Force would acquire a new and vibrant dimension that would also revive a noble military tradition. At the same time, NASA would be liberated from an overcommitment to management of large programs that often smother its primary pathfinding role. Henceforth, NASA's mission would be to keep probing at the space frontier, throwing out new challenges for science, conceiving and designing manned missions. Thus, the Air Force would be the chief operational agent for manned activities of a civilian-directed space exploration program.

Something similar occurred under Apollo. The operational director of Apollo was an Air Force general detailed to NASA. A

* The testing of space weapons systems components will bring humans into space for a while. But an operational SDI, as currently envisioned, will be run from underground.

large proportion of the mission control staff were Air Force officers who exchanged their blue uniforms for civvies in order to keep up the "civilian" image. All the astronauts were either military pilots or former military pilots. The Air Force tracked the astronauts in orbit, and the Navy picked them up at splashdown. Apollo owed as much to the Air Force as it did to NASA—but split-perception blocked us from seeing it.

Well, it's time to stop playing these self-denying games. In the Soviet Union, manned space flight is already run by the military. If we are to coordinate operationally with them, as the Space Age demands, who would be better suited on our side than the Air Force? For everyone's sake, including its own, America's winged service should climb out of its underground bunker and join a great united effort to explore far-off new worlds.

10 / NEW SPACE FOR AMERICAN INDUSTRY

I hadn't expected to propose a new Space Age mission for the Air Force when I began working on the military space symposium speech—it just unfolded as I reexamined the Air Force mission from a Space Age perspective.

Something similar occurred when I considered the potential Space Age role of the other large segment of the military space symposium audience—the aerospace industry. For American high-tech industry, especially aerospace, DOD and NASA are interchangeable markets. When NASA commissioned preliminary design studies for a space station, it turned to McDonnell Douglas, Boeing, Rockwell International, Grumman, General Dynamics, Lockheed—the builders of Trident submarines, Polaris missiles, B-1 bombers, and F-16 fighters. Those companies sold more to DOD than to NASA, not because they preferred making weapons, but because the U.S. government preferred buying weapons. During the Apollo program of the 1960s, which at its peak generated 400,000 high-tech jobs, our aerospace "weapons" industry was on the way to becoming a space exploration industry.

That interchangeability has particular significance for the critical and often overriding issue of defense-industry jobs. When the phasing out or reduction of a weapons system means that thousands of American families in several states might be left without a source of income, the congressional representatives from those states have legitimate cause for concern. These workers aren't warmongers. They must, however, provide for their families. The result is that, for reasons having nothing to do with the Soviet threat but everything to do with the basic needs of their constituents, members of Congress often feel compelled to give the Pentagon even more weapons than it requests. It's all part of the cold war's closed loop of insanity. Large chunks of the economy are trapped in it.

Related to the defense-jobs issue is what military planners call the defense industrial base. In order to be ready for a national emergency, DOD believes it has to protect the health of key segments of high-tech industry by keeping them busy with a steady stream of defense contracts. It is ironic that the need to protect the industrial base grows more urgent when U.S.–U.S.S.R. relations improve and the defense budget faces possible reductions: whether or not we need weapons now, we need a healthy industrial base to produce weapons later. The way to keep it healthy is to produce weapons now.

At that point in my reflections, I recalled the ongoing national debate about industrial policy. Industrial policy means targeting key industries for development with government support. Activist Democrats generally favor it. Republicans generally oppose it as requiring too much government intervention in the economy. But the truth is that we already have a gargantuan industrial policy and it is a favorite of Republicans, although they don't recognize it because it goes by another name. It is called defense procurement. At least, unlike some Democratic policies, defense procurement has the virtue of supporting high-tech industrial production, but it nonetheless needs to be recognized for what it is: a defense industrial policy in which federal support for high-tech productivity and innovation is channeled through weapons spending. Under that policy, DOD research and development is activated not only to meet national security threats but also to meet purely economic threats.

Our defense industrial policy thus deserves comparison with alternatives developed by economic competitors; notably, Japan. For instance, the United States has responded to the Japanese challenge for the next generation of high-speed computers by turning to the U.S. agent for industrial policy—DOD—and giving it special funding for high-speed-computer research. The Japanese, on the other hand, have vested their effort with MITI, their vaunted Ministry of Trade and Industry. The difference between MITI and DOD is, essentially, the difference between Japanese and U.S. industrial policy. Besides being weapons-oriented, the DOD effort is constrained by an institutional commitment to secrecy. Meanwhile, MITI focuses single-mindedly on the open market. MITI's idea of competitiveness is to develop products of superior quality at lower prices to compete for world markets. DOD's idea of competitiveness is to win a competition with the Soviet military at any cost. MITI's whole orientation is outward toward economically competitive *production* for the market. DOD is oriented inward, toward *consumption* of products produced in a non-economic competition.

There is, of course, the spin-off factor, in which weapons research leads eventually to civilian products. But in the faster and faster moving high-tech world, where products often become obsolete in a year or two, or even within a few months, the delay from secrecy-shrouded weapons production to the spin-offs for free market competition can be deadly. Too often, by the time defense spin-offs reach the market, they've been left behind by competitors whose research and development efforts are aimed directly at that market. The main thing that keeps the spin-off factor viable today is the vast sum of money we keep pouring into weapons research that allows DOD to dominate certain fields. But that has nothing to do with efficiency, productivity, or economic competitiveness, and it could come back to haunt us.

The bottom line is that the chief consumer of the technologies and products developed by DOD is DOD, which makes DOD, to put it mildly, an inefficient instrument of industrial policy. How will our reliance on DOD high-tech consumption affect American competitiveness in the 1990s, when the commercial fruits of two fundamentally different high-tech industrial policies will really take effect? Already, the trends in our economy are running dangerously from outward production to inward consumption. By drawing American high-tech industry into a massive *non-economic* competition with the Soviets, while expecting that same industry to remain economically competitive with the Japanese and others, our defense industrial policy is making those trends worse.

We need to pay more attention to the non-economic competition factor on the defense technology frontier. No matter how successful the effort to eliminate $2,000 socket wrenches and $7,000 toilet seats, we will still be faced with the fact that DOD procurement is often a deliberate exercise in sheerest fantasy. DOD procurement officers don't design or build weapons. Instead, they dream up "requirements"—say, a missile mounted on an F-16 fighter-bomber which can seek out and hit a manhole cover at a distance of a thousand miles. Private contractors then set to work designing the "required" dream product for its trillionaire customer, DOD, and costs take off from there. They are kept in orbit by the key "requirement" for our weapons systems, which is to maintain "technological superiority" over the Soviets which will offset numerical inferiority. But how much technological superiority is enough? No one really knows. So defense procurers go after all they can get for all the money they can get.

To make matters worse, the strategists of technological superiority have concluded that virtually any kind of technological superiority is worthwhile if it diverts Soviet resources into developing responses to it. In a sense, it amounts to a bizarre new military mission: develop high-tech products the enemy must counter at great expense. Military tactics and strategy are adjusted to this new mission, as are industrial efficiency, productivity, and competitiveness. Instead of devising operational deployments, our military planners devise procurement deployments for weapons whose mission is technological superiority. This is pure abstraction. As for cost—who can put a price on national security when it is redefined as a limitless quest for new technologies?

If we follow that suicidal course long enough, the winner of the cold war will be Japan. While we are furiously forcing the Soviets into successive phases of technological inferiority, the Japanese (and others) are directing their high-tech efforts toward winning the competition for markets around the world, including our own domestic market. Meanwhile, our defense industrial policy is producing weapons systems in competition with the Soviets, but with no Soviet market as a reward for success.

Even in weapons sales to other nations, the U.S. is already losing its advantages as France, Britain, Israel, West Germany, and others become more competitive for the military equipment that most nations want, such as combat vehicles and light weapons. But who besides the American taxpayers will buy a laser battle station? As a result of our all-consuming pursuit of "technological superiority," American economic productivity and competitiveness are locked into a competition that undermines American productivity and competitiveness.

Significantly, no comparable danger exists for the Soviets. Whether the Japanese, the West Germans, or the Koreans are ahead or behind in computers or semiconductors is of minimal concern to the ruling Soviet bureaucracy. Why should it be? The key to Soviet efficiency, such as it is, lies in the rejection of democratic rules of the marketplace in favor of an authoritarian regime that decides who gets what, no questions asked. The more we squeeze them, the more we strengthen the authoritarianism at the root of their own politically distorted brand of economic efficiency. So we force them to divert more funds to military spending? A strong balanced economy, offering a wider variety of consumer choices, could do no good for Soviet authoritarianism; but it might—and probably would—enhance democratic inclinations. Military spending creates no such problems.

American military strength is built upon free-enterprise competitiveness in a global economy. The Soviet economic system has no comparable base. Somehow, we have to restructure the competition with the Soviets so that the price of victory won't be the defeat of American industry abroad and the imposition of a national security state at home. If we fail to take corrective measures, the entire structure of American society will be threatened. We can't forget that the model national-security state is the Soviet Union.

And that's where space comes in. Only space offers an arena, a theme, and an organizing principle grand enough to liberate us from the closed loop of insanity that has ensnared us. We *do* need an industrial policy that fosters leading-edge high technology, that's product-oriented, that strengthens our industrial base, insures the strongest defense, delivers commercial products, and enhances American competitiveness. But if high-tech space and defense are the two interchangeable conduits for those objectives, we would be far more successful in achieving our aims by establishing space as a theater of joint activity:

• Joint activity in space means international joint ventures of the sort that American high-tech companies require to improve productivity and competitiveness. For instance, in a major U.S.–U.S.S.R.–Europe–Japan space project, American industry could apply its superior management skills to putting together winning combinations of companies for the project's giant contracts. At the same time, Soviet managers would come under enormous pressure to open up their system in order to compete. Joint activity in space means *open competition*, which is inherently democratizing and favors free enterprise, rather than *secretive competition*, which leads, as we shall see, to an expansion of government control in whatever society is drawn into it.

• Space is an ideal frontier for reasserting American competitiveness. The Japanese and others have equaled or passed us in high-tech services delivered by mass production—from TV sets to transistors. But space is different. Mass-production economies of scale weren't major factors in the Apollo moon program. Instead, the emphasis was on the integration of a small number of very large systems. The Japanese are still a generation away from producing anything like Apollo, which we have already left a generation behind. We envy Japanese techniques for mass production of consumer products. They envy our ability to integrate large-scale space systems.

• Space is more responsive to American innovative instincts. The Japanese, a confined island people, have developed into fine tuners par excellence almost by historical necessity. By contrast, American genius works best when it has room. American ingenuity thrives in the expansive physical environment of a new frontier. Today, only space offers the kinds of challenges that initially defined the character of American industry—and put us on top.

• Alas, our current major venture in space is the Strategic Defense Initiative. Besides their other enumerated defects, space weapons are a poor space investment. That might not seem obvious immediately because we're throwing so much money into space-weapons research—$26 billion in five years. But it's as nutritious for our economic health as a bowl of chocolate syrup.

The fifteen-to-twenty-year timetable from Star Wars research to full deployment will mean new secrecy restrictions for American research at the high-tech frontier. That cloak of control will grow as systems integration pulls in more and more segments of high-tech industry. It would be a defense industrial policy carried to the furthest extreme, with all its defects magnified, with free-enterprise access to the fruits of our investment increasingly limited. Already, DOD's share of all federally funded research has jumped to seventy percent, and twenty percent of that research is so secret the American people don't even know that it exists.

How can American high-tech industry compete under those conditions? In place of Space Age free enterprise, we'll have government bureaucracies writing the high-tech contracts and controlling the product. Competition will mean "competing" around a government trough whose importance will magnify as the global competitiveness of American industry declines and the dependence on government procurement increases. A space-weapons race will lead America away from free competition and toward authoritarian Big Government at its worst.

Finally, despite its trillion-dollar cost which would drain funds from other Space Age activities, the *product* will have no constructive economic application and might not even work. Space-weapons systems won't provide infrastructure or constitute stepping-stones for space exploration and settlement. They will just sit up there in space, a trillion-dollar building block to nowhere.

• On the other hand, a space station and related activities would fit neatly into the successful context for federal support of emerging industries: it would be the basis for development on the next frontier—like the first roads spanning the continent built by U.S. Army engineers. In keeping with the unique technological challenge of that frontier, it would also be an active research laboratory for production of materials for use on earth. (What would space-weapons systems produce in space?) And it would serve as a launch platform for interplanetary missions. It thus has direct Space Age utility, aside from the many spin-offs that would accrue from its design, construction, and operation.

• The space station and most other space projects point toward the international joint ventures American high-tech industry needs to retain global competitiveness. That's the difference between secret and open applications of aerospace industry skills. Open applications have the advantage of at once encouraging cooperation and *open* competition. They would establish the competitive environment which created American private enterprise and which is still its greatest source of strength, especially on the high-tech frontier. No nation on this planet can match the skill, originality, and productive genius of America's diverse network of university research institutions working in alliance with high-tech industry and guided by a cultural commitment to rapid, open communication. Instead of closing down communication and compartmentalizing secretive research, thus bottling up those unique powers on the space frontier, we should be unleashing them. Then no one can catch us.

• It's a dangerous delusion to believe we can proceed on our present course and still draw on America's unique creative dynamism. A space station will cost $8 billion by the time it's constructed in 1993 or thereabouts. Beyond that, there is the possibility of a manned Mars mission ($40 billion) sometime in the next century. But by then we would have spent several *hundred billion* dollars on Star Wars. Space technology development would be ruled by secrecy-ridden national-security considerations. The opportunities for meaningful joint activity in an openly competitive environment, modeled after the United States, would be choked off. Instead, the Soviet economic style of oppressive controls would be the international model for development on the space frontier. We are already approaching that point.

By the time I completed a final draft of my remarks for the military space symposium, I had covered some most unexpected terrain. But it was all a matter of perspective. The activities I proposed were in the same category as the federal support that we, and all nations, had given to development on our land frontiers. The only difference was that space infrastructure (space stations, manned and unmanned interplanetary probes) would take many more years to pay dividends commensurate to the investment. That's the character of the Space Age—the age of long lead times and new perceptions. It helps explain the imperative need for nations to coordinate their work on the highways of space, and it suggests the profits that American industry and American values will reap from such coordination.

To my chagrin, a Senate–House conference committee meeting on the tax bill prevented me from addressing the military space symposium personally. So I sent my legislative counselor, Harvey Meyerson, to read the twenty-five-page text. The next day, I asked him how the audience responded.

"They seemed stunned, Senator," he said.

Well, so was I—by the possibilities the Space Age really offered if we gave it a chance.

11 / CREEPING SECRECY

During the early years of the cold war, C. P. Snow, the late British novelist and dean of science policy-makers, warned against the dangers of secrecy in government. "The euphoria of secrecy," wrote Lord Snow, "goes to the head very much like the euphoria for gadgets . . . It takes a very strong head to keep secrets for years and not go slightly mad." We have been at it for more than a generation since Lord Snow issued his warning, and the national secrecy apparatus keeps growing at the expense of freedom.

The doctrine of technological superiority has carried secrecy controls into every aspect of high-tech commerce and is making it increasingly difficult for a businessman to know exactly what is or isn't a restricted "national security" commodity. Moreover, the most forceful *administrator* of high-tech export controls, the Department of Defense, is also the largest single *purchaser* of high-tech products, to the tune of hundreds of billions of dollars. If you're competing for DOD business, it might not be wise to complain too much about secrecy controls.

The oppressive secrecy net is also expanding into what Lewis

Thomas calls "the most communal of human endeavors," basic scientific research. In the logic of the cold war's closed loop of insanity, ever greater restrictions on scientific research make sense. Even more valuable to our adversary than a computer would be the know-how to manufacture that computer. But where does the know-how begin? What is its source? Gradually, the secrecy net has reached out from applied technology to technology research, and from there it is edging into basic research.

There has been no shortage of reaction. Each new intrusion brings public protests. Professional societies document and condemn encroaching secrecy. Presidents of prestigious universities voice their concerns. Congress holds hearings. Nobel laureates sign petitions. Nor are those reactions ignored by secrecy-makers. They convene advisory panels and numerous special meetings. Secrecy edicts are often revised and made less stringent, to widespread approval. And yet, despite all that, secrecy continues to grow. Secrecy administrators advance until they hit a point of excess; whereupon critics "reform" them; whereupon, revised and renewed, they resume their steady advance.

Secrecy wars have even broken out between federal agencies over which is more reliable at protecting secrets and established restrictive controls over Americans in an effort to make life more difficult for Russians. When the Department of Defense complained that the Commerce Department was lax in enforcing export controls, Commerce struck back. In February 1985, Commerce Secretary Malcolm Baldridge charged DOD, State, NASA, and the Energy Department with "tolerating a massive giveaway program" of secrets that included "much the same type of technologies and products that the Administration is trying to keep out of Soviet hands through the multilateral export control system." Baldridge was talking about thousands of technical papers that remained in the public domain. He was calling for a massive new program of classification of public documents that would no doubt be followed by more stringent rules for classification, extending secrecy's reach still further into the most communal and open of human endeavors.

That potentially devastating trend toward ever-greater secrecy, which would cripple efficiency as well as freedom (as the Soviet Union has proved so well), can only accelerate with an all-out commitment to the Strategic Defense Initiative. Because Star Wars is to a considerable extent a mission in search of a weapon, and because that search has been cast so wide that it practically blanketed the high-tech frontier, space-weapons research poses an unprecedented threat to the character of high-tech research—all the more dangerous because it is masked as a seduction. Under the new priorities, increased funding for space-weapons research has been coupled with decreased funding for civilian research. Star Wars then waves its megabucks at the scientists it has effectively starved.

Thus, national security statism encroaches steadily into the fields of science, commerce, research, trade, competitiveness, and freedom.

Hints of still another offshoot of the secrecy trend, which reached out even more ominously into the lives of millions of Americans, appeared in the fall of 1983 in testimony at a U.S. House of Representatives hearing by Professor George Davida of the Department of Electrical Engineering, University of Wisconsin at Milwaukee. Dr. Davida testified in connection with his research into devices to protect theft of information from home and business computers. He felt compelled to speak out after his research activities were intruded upon by the National Security Agency. As part of its responsibility for electronic surveillance of foreign nations, notably the U.S.S.R., the super-secretive NSA had decided that it must have "technological superiority" over any mechanical device that any American citizen used to protect his or her privacy at home. NSA agents had intruded on Dr. Davida's work in that field. They didn't want him to get ahead of them. He testified about the implications: "Our nation is changing. The most intimate details of our lives are being stored and manipulated by computers.

Medical data bases, credit files, insurance files, employment records are being constructed and connected to computer networks . . . These technological changes can potentially destroy not just privacy, which is already gravely threatened, but freedom itself. It is difficult to conceive of freedom without privacy."

Dr. Davida's references to privacy and freedom raise a provocative point. In a totalitarian society, individual citizens have virtually no privacy rights and the state has unlimited privacy rights; that is, the state has the right to know anything it wants about its individual citizens, while those citizens have no rights to know anything about the state. In a democracy, the situation is—or is supposed to be—the reverse. Knowledge is power, and in a democracy it is supposed to belong to the people. America's Founding Fathers took special pains to protect individual privacy and to insure that the activities of government remained open to public scrutiny. The cold war is reordering those fundamental democratic priorities. Government secrecy is gaining at the expense of individual privacy. Individual freedom is losing out to state control.

The implications of Dr. Davida's testimony seem even more ominous in the light of National Security Decision Directive 145, issued in April 1985, which calls for a program to increase computer and telecommunications security within our borders that would cost billions of dollars. The program would be administered principally by the National Security Agency, the most secretive of all government agencies. An NSA spokesman said that the new directive "broadens both the communications and computer security missions of this agency," by involving NSA in a program of domestic surveillance of unprecedented scope. NSA would henceforth have the power to tap into private lines of communication used by millions of Americans.

The rationale is that NSA has the expertise. But the rationale ignores the personality of NSA. An agency's personality—any agency—is determined by its mission. Members of NSA are probably no more fanatical about secret surveillance than car salesmen are about selling cars or doctors about curing illness. One might even say that they are conscientious about surveillance. But they pursue their responsibilities under a special burden. They see themselves as being caught up in a struggle with a ruthless adversary, in an unbreaking sequence of move and countermove, in which secrecy is life and openness death. Others talk of the threat of war. To them, unceasing secret war is the condition of existence, the overriding reality. Under that condition, it is difficult if not impossible for secrecy experts to step back and perceive the effect of their activities on their own nation's values and institutions. Hitler said that the ultimate weapon of totalitarian states was that they forced their enemies to imitate them. In the name of efficiency—as part of the continuing effort to block out every possible avenue of access for Soviet spies—super-secretive NSA is being led toward endless new forms of domestic surveillance that threaten the fabric of the society NSA is fighting to protect.

Again, it's the trend that bothers me. Major changes won't occur suddenly. But so long as the gradual trend is toward greater government secrecy and greater government intrusion in private lives, our nation is retreating from its democratic heritage. Whether that retreat is for a noble cause or not, the result will be the same: the very gradual development of a systematic network of state surveillance and control. While dismantling the apparatus of Big Government in the name of freedom, we are replacing it with the apparatus of Big Brother in the name of security.

As a first step toward correcting that self-consuming process, we must recognize the full implications of a line of reasoning that goes something like this: in conducting the cold war, Soviet totalitarianism has certain important advantages over American democracy. The Soviet government isn't accountable to the Soviet people. The Soviet media is tightly controlled. The activities of Soviet scholars, technicians, and other professionals are tightly controlled. Secrecy prevails at every level. For the sake of national survival, we must respond in kind.

That line of reasoning invites cold-war policies and strategies based on the assumption that the chief weakness of democracy is—democracy. It is thus a luxury available only to those removed from the struggle. But since the Soviets are carrying the struggle into American education, science, free enterprise, government, you name it, then in those ever-increasing number of cases, democracy must be sacrificed.

Congressional oversight of surveillance activities, although necessary, isn't enough to halt that ominous trend. In addition to restraints, which only slow down the process without stopping it, we need policies that actively employ democratic openness as a weapon in the cold war.

And what better point to begin than with the NSA itself. In one of the typically paradoxical ironies of the cold war, we are employing the most powerful Space Age instrument for democratic openness for the most secretive mission ever conceived. That instrument is secret satellite surveillance administered by the NSA. The combination of satellite technology and the panoramic view from space offers a unified *open* view of our planet such as civilization has never known. Why not maximize its potential? Dwight Eisenhower pointed the way with his "open skies" proposal of the 1950s, by which the U.S. and the U.S.S.R. would have traded aerial surveillance photos of each other's terrain. France took the idea a step further in the 1970s with a proposal for an international satellite-monitoring agency.

I would suggest combining aspects of those two proposals by having individual nations coordinate their separate surveillance activities, with NSA serving as our lead Open Skies agency. A new Open Skies policy could be used for global drought prediction, crop management, pollution control, and a host of other environmental-protection services that our planet badly needs. Farther down the road, Open Skies agencies might publish military strengths and movements worldwide. There would be resistance; implementation would be extremely difficult and complex and would occur in gradual stages, but at least in pushing for it we would give the offensive to democratic openness.*

Another way of restoring the offensive to democracy occurred to me while pondering how to respond to a long-awaited invitation from Air Force Major Ellison Onizuka. Onizuka was America's first astronaut of Asian ancestry and he was from Hawaii. I had known his family for years. They were fine people. I had followed young Ellison's Air Force career almost with pride of family as he moved up quickly through the ranks to a coveted position in the astronaut corps and a slot on a shuttle mission scheduled for January 1985. At his request, I had arranged for him to receive the banner of the 100th Battalion, so that it might be unfurled in space during Ellison's first shuttle flight, in honor of my comrades-in-arms who had died during World War II. Rarely had I looked forward to an event with greater anticipation. I planned to fly down to Cape Canaveral for the shuttle launching.

Then I received the shocking news that Ellison's shuttle flight was to be America's first secret shuttle mission. It was almost too much to bear. This magnificent young man was to make his debut in space on a mission whose guiding principle I abhorred. I couldn't— and didn't—attend the launch. The secret event wasn't televised, of course, and no one saw the 100th Battalion banner unfurled, or even knew about it. The space mission I longed to witness had been blacked out.

The secret shuttle dramatized another dangerous trend. In 1982, the DOD space budget exceeded NASA's for the first time. In 1983, we initiated a space-weapons program that would cost hundreds of billions of dollars. In January 1985, we launched the first totally

---

* *Admiral Stansfield Turner, former director of the Central Intelligence Agency, proposes an Open Skies mission for NSA in his book* Secrecy and Democracy. *Howard G. Kurtz and his late wife, Harriet, pursued the international satellite-monitoring theme for years in Washington, with quiet grace and persistence.*

secret manned space mission. Could anyone doubt where this was leading? Like everything else in our closed loop of insanity, the worst choice kept being presented as the only choice.

In an effort to argue the need for an alternative context, and offer one, I drafted an article and submitted it to *The New York Times*, in time for it to appear at the conclusion of the first secret shuttle launch. I wrote, in part:

The now-you-see-it now-you-don't space shuttle has come down to earth. We know it was up there because we saw it take off, then land. The rest is unknown, except to the American and Soviet military specialists who, hand-in-hand so to speak, secretly tracked the secret mission . . .

"The most powerful nation on earth is a poor helpless creature of events," we are told. "The Soviets have used their manned space program for secret activities for years. We have to 'match' them or democracy will be destroyed."

But if we continue on the course we are headed, we may wind up saving the Soviets the trouble.

At its root, the principal difference between the U.S. and the U.S.S.R. is that we are an open society and they are a closed society. To the extent that they open up, they become more like us; to the extent that we close down, we become more like them.

So far, they hold the initiative. We merely tag along, pleading helplessness. It seems to me that the leader of the Free World can do better.

The Soviets are forcing our manned spaceflight program into darkness?

Then *take the initiative* and propose that all manned spaceflight be conducted on an open basis. Since that has been our consistent policy for a generation (until January 23, 1985), we would stand to gain far more than the Soviets from such an agreement. To meet its terms, they would have to open up their manned program, i.e., democratize.

105

The Soviets may one day force us to use our space station for secret military activities?

Then take the initiative and propose that space-station activities be made open and cooperative . . .

The article was rejected. But on the Sunday preceding the flight, *The New York Times Magazine* carried an article reporting that the shuttle's secret cargo was the most advanced model of a spy-in-the-sky satellite. The writer described how the shuttle itself might be used for aerial spying. He left the reader on the launch-pad, "waiting to open the newest frontier in espionage."

That's where the euphoria of secrecy described by Lord Snow a generation ago has carried us. We can and must do better on the space frontier, find ways to be creative instead of reactive, and stop copying the Soviets.

12 / TOWARD GLOBALISM

During the months of intense involvement with the space cooperation resolution, most of my regular Senate activity centered on the tariff and tax-writing Finance Committee where I served. But even there the Space Age perspective made a difference, especially during the committee's lengthy consideration of the Export Administration Act, or EAA.

The Export Administration Act was a product of the cold war, pure and simple. It neither protected established American industry nor encouraged new industry. In fact, it was an export bill *against exports*. Its purpose was to control them for reasons of U.S. national security and foreign policy.

The EAA's history was revealing. Congress passed the first EAA in 1969, just six years after I came to Washington as a member of the House of Representatives. Its purpose, at the time, was to *increase* exports to the Soviet bloc. Since the early 1950s, we had maintained a virtual embargo on trade with the Soviet Union. By 1969, however, other Western nations were expanding trade with the Soviet bloc and our embargo no longer made sense. The EAA of 1969 opened up trade, except for banning exports that made a "significant contribution to the military potential" of the U.S.S.R. and other unfriendly countries.

But as the years passed, it began to seem as if we had merely opened the door to a labyrinth. Just what contributed to military potential? Definitions proliferated—and forms for businessmen to fill out—and delays. Then, when the national security controls rule book began to sink under its own weight, we set about "reforming" it, "streamlining" regulations, setting up new and more precise categories, refining them, seeing them proliferate all over again, and so on.

The United States application of national security export controls became more stringent, fickle, and complex than that of any other nation. Although our policy was aimed at the Soviet Union, it also controlled U.S. exports to any nation that might possibly trade with the Soviet bloc or (twice removed) any nation that might trade with nations that traded with the Soviet bloc. In order to maintain technological superiority over the Soviets, we restricted our high-tech trade with everyone.

How was that campaign to control our high-tech exports working? What was its effect on American competitiveness worldwide? Four out of five new U.S. manufacturing jobs were in export-related industries, and nearly half our exports consisted of high-tech goods and services. The Japanese, Taiwanese, Koreans, and others had moved up or passed us in light and heavy industry, *except* at the leading edge of high technology. That was our strongest suit. Fully a quarter of our computer industry's sales were overseas, and other high-tech manufacturers were equally dependent on foreign sales. For American high-tech industry, trade was a matter of survival.

I had queried the scientific community, and I now turned to the business community. In order to better assess the long-term impact of export-control policies on American industry, I sent letters to the chief executive officers of America's major high-tech exporters, based on rankings by *Fortune* magazine and the American Electronics Association. Among the questions I asked:

"What, if any, are your major concerns regarding the evolution of U.S. export policy?"

"In your view, to what extent, if any, might export sanctions affect the development of high technology industry in the United States?"

The replies provided a short course in how a free-enterprise society, built on competition, could willfully undermine its competitiveness.

Roy Anderson, chairman of Lockheed Aircraft: "U.S. export controls are currently framed and implemented as if the U.S. still dominated the international field of high technology . . . In reality, we face intense, accelerating competition in high technology from several foreign suppliers."

Carl Danta, president of Compugraphic Corp.: "Given the high development costs and relatively short life cycles of these [computer] products, it is critical for American manufacturers to have access to a broad international marketplace."

Allen E. Pucket, chairman and CEO of Hughes Aircraft: "Our world is highly competitive and everywhere I have witnessed enormous national drives by other countries to get into the business of high technology . . . If we are unable to supply our foreign markets, our competitors will undoubtedly accelerate their own technological skills, and will in time replace us in those markets."

Sanford N. McDonnell, chairman and CEO of McDonnell Douglas: "With technologies advancing at such a rapid rate both within the United States and in the overseas marketplace, it is very difficult even for the most aggressive, intelligent and dynamic members of the bureaucracy to have a current understanding of that which is in fact a transfer of technology."

L. W. Lehr, chairman and CEO of Minnesota Mining and Manufacturing, after noting that one of every three U.S. jobs at 3M depended on international business: "Trade can't be turned on and off like a faucet; once American companies get the reputation of being unreliable suppliers, it can take years to turn that reputation around—and in the interim, business is lost to competitors from other countries."

James Litton, Jr., senior vice-president and general manager, Magnavox: "If present trends continue, we will begin to see U.S. home markets for advanced equipment flooded by foreign products from foreign companies grown strong on business diverted to them by U.S. government action against U.S. companies."

Edward G. Law, director of Export Regulation, IBM: "Large international joint ventures are becoming increasingly important to future growth. Foreign corporations, who are the potential partners in these joint ventures, and their governments are becoming very skeptical about accepting American partners."

Led by high technology, something *global* was occurring. From its earliest beginnings, commerce had fostered interdependence. Now Space Age high technology was carrying commerce beyond interdependence and toward international joint ventures that enhanced productivity and competitiveness. Joint venturing wasn't the rule. It was a trend—a pressure—felt by high-tech industry.

As in politics, two trends competed in the economic sector—two opposing inevitabilities, as it were. On one side were restrictive export controls; on the other, expansive joint ventures. One led toward democratic openness and free market competition; the other, toward authoritarian secrecy and state control.

And, as in politics, space weapons loomed as a decisive factor in determining which economic trend would win out. At about the time I was collecting correspondence from American business, Dr. George Keyworth, the President's Science Adviser, testified before the Senate Foreign Relations Committee on the role of computers in the Strategic Defense Initiative. Civilian computer research "inevitably" leads to space weapons, Dr. Keyworth explained, because computers "will be at the heart of any defense against ballistic missiles." Thus, space weapons "are a natural by-product of our civilian industries and universities." All roads, it seems, lead to weapons, secrecy, and state control.

Dr. Keyworth's self-perpetuating "inevitability" explains the growing influence of a concept called dual use. Dual-use technologies have both civilian and military applications. According to an article in the NATO Science and Society newsletter, expanding dual use results from "the increasing dependence of military systems on the common advanced technological base of our modern societies." Since military applications take precedence in a cold war that is becoming permanent, the result can only be a steadily increasing militarization of activities at the high-tech frontier. It is as if the steam engine, the telephone, the light bulb, the Bessemer steelmaking process, had all been defined as militarily critical technologies upon their discovery and their development had been controlled by a secretive government bureaucracy.

One by one, we are turning off the lights on the high-tech frontier. Efforts to streamline the control mechanisms might slow the process down, but they can't stop it. Slowly, inexorably, we are approaching that cross-over point where wartime industry conditions comparable to World War II will operate in peacetime—we will live in a permanent war economy.

The crowning point is the primary emphasis the control process places, as Dr. Keyworth noted, on information technology. There, too, the implications extend beyond—far beyond—technology transfer. Whoever controls the transfer of information technology will also, ultimately, control the transfer of information—the lifeblood of democracy. Under that inevitability, it is only a matter of time before democracy itself poses a threat to national security.

But we can't see it. The cold war has imposed perceptions whose unprecedented narrowness distorts every viewpoint. Broad-minded people are judged narrow and vice versa. Scientists who seek to protect the international character of their profession are said to ignore the "big picture" of the cold war. Similarly, businessmen who seek expanded trade are said to be ruled only by narrow profit motives which ignore the "larger" requirements of the cold war, although commerce predates the cold war by several thousand years and has been one of the most persistently civilizing and democratizing forces in human history. The real truth is that the cold-war "big picture" is a black hole.

During the fall of 1982, when I was first trying to reach beyond the limited context that had guided my thoughts, I came upon an article in *The New York Times* by the remarkable Isaac Asimov, visionary scientist, novelist, historian, and unmatched explicator. The article, which I clipped and consulted frequently for inspiration, examined the legacy of the Space Age so far. "If I can put it into one word," wrote Asimov, "it is globalism." He went on to describe how, materially and psychologically, the Space Age had "forced into our unwilling minds . . . a view that presents Earth and humanity as a single entity." Asimov wrote a letter of support for my space cooperation resolution shortly after it was introduced. Now, impulsively, I decided to write a letter asking him to expand his views.

Asimov's response was both generous and enlightening—an essay on the history of civilization and its prospects in the Space Age. He explained how, in the past, war had served as a force both for unity and for division, since it was used alternately to build empires and to pull them down. Traditionally, a confrontation comparable to the current one between the United States and the Soviet Union, Asimov wrote, would have been resolved by war, leading to a greater empire, followed in due course by its fragmentation. But now everything had changed. By introducing the prospect of global annihilation, the nuclear age posed an unprecedented dilemma. Isaac Asimov described it and proposed a solution:

There must be world unification—yet it would seem that there can't be world unification. We can't force world unification by war, because we chiefly need world unification to *prevent* war . . . How can we reconcile the irreconcilables?

History may seem to make such a task unlikely of fulfillment. The Francophones of Quebec are still fighting the English victory of two and a half centuries ago; the Catholics of Northern Ireland are still fighting the English victory of three centuries ago; the Israelis are defending a land they last defended nineteen centuries ago. Nothing seems forgettable. And yet there is an example of the contrary also.

In the American Civil War, the Southern states, after heroic and resolute battle, were defeated and humiliated. The "Lost Cause" is not forgotten in the South, but the bitterness is gone. There are no Confederates still fighting for independence by guerrilla war and terrorism. What happened?

In the decades following the Civil War, the Western territories of the United States were opened and converted into states. People flooded Westward from North and South alike, from the victors and from the defeated. In the great common task of building a greater nation, the petty passions of the past, if not forgotten, were seen at least in better perspective and lost their importance.

Can we then, in similar fashion, find a great project in which the nations of the world—the Soviet Union and the United States, in particular—can learn to disregard their differences in similar fashion?

It would help if we could find something that all nations held in common. To be sure, we hold our biology in common. All of us, wherever our culture, form a single species, entirely capable of interbreeding and of understanding each other intellectually. We have all developed language, art, and religion.

However, the superficial differences of appearance of skin, eyes, hair, noses, height, and so on are so noticeable that the common biology is all too often forgotten, even though the similarities among us are enormously greater than the differences.

Differences in culture, although even more superficial (after all, an American-born Chinese child can become completely American in all aspects of culture, and a Chinese-born American child can become completely Chinese), are even more productive of hatred and suspicion. Differences in language and religion, in eating habits, in superstitions and customs, in notions of family, in the subtle manner of social intercourse, all seem to set us irreconcilably apart.

And yet there is one aspect of humanity which is identical everywhere—science and technology.

Modern science may have been developed in Western Europe, but it has spread through the whole world and there is no competitor. There is no such thing as Japanese science or Nigerian science or Paraguayan science, each based on a different set of axioms, following distinctive laws of logic, and producing totally distinct varieties of solutions to identical problems, taking advantage of mutually exclusive laws of nature.

The laws of thermodynamics, quantum theory, the principle of indeterminacy, the conservation laws, the concepts of relativity and of biological evolution, the findings of astronomy and chemistry, are the same everywhere, and people of all nations and cultures can (and do) contribute to their further elaboration and application. Airplanes fly for all of us, television sets entertain, antibiotics cure, and nuclear bombs explode. For that matter, we all use the same resources and produce the same pollutants.

Can we not take advantage of the science and technology that humanity holds in common to find some acceptable ground on which we can all stand?

For instance, the most dramatic advance we have made in the last generation has been our advance into space. Once again, humanity has opened the possibility for a splendid increase of range, one that even surpasses the last great advance of the "Age of Exploration" four centuries ago. Human beings have stood on the Moon and human instruments have examined at close range worlds as far as Saturn.

The possibilities to which this extension of range can give rise are enormous . . . We can mine the Moon and, later, the asteroids for the material necessary to build structures in space. We can build observatories in space that can study the Universe undisturbed by our troublesome atmosphere. We can build laboratories in which to conduct experiments too dangerous for intimate contact with Earth's biosphere. We can build factories that will take advantage of the unusal properites of space (zero gravity, hard radiation, low temperatures, endless vacuum) to do things that can be done with difficulty, or not at all, on Earth. We can transfer our industrial plant, as much as possible, into orbit and free the planet of much of its pollutants. We can even build cities in space and develop new societies.

Clearly, all of this can benefit all nations, all peoples, alike . . . How criminal it would be of us not to seize the opportunity, and to use space only as an arena for extending the threat and practice of war . . .

And yet simply to speak grandiosely of space and of the extension of the human range in general is to risk drowning in generalities.

Where do we begin? What specific task can we undertake and make into a cooperative venture? And if worldwide cooperation is not in the cards, what type of lesser cooperation might serve as a first step?

I suppose that no one would argue the fact that by far the most dangerous rivalry in the world today is that between the United States and the Soviet Union. Whatever destruction other rivalries may bring about, only a full-scale war between the two superpowers can bring about the final Armageddon.

It would therefore be in the highest degree useful if we can bring about some joint Soviet–American venture of note and drama, which can engage the full attention of the world, and to which other nations can contribute if they wish . . .

The Moon is reachable and has been reached, and Mars is the next nearest world on which human beings could stand. (Venus, which is somewhat closer, has a temperature and atmospheric density that cannot, at the present level of technology, conceivably be endured by astronauts.)

To send a human expedition to Mars is, at present, something that is at the extreme range of human capability. If we can carry it off, however, the knowledge gained could be extraordinarily useful, for Mars is the most Earth-like planet (other than Earth itself) in the solar system, and is yet significantly different. Quite apart from the usefulness of the project, the drama should catch the emotions and the imaginations of humanity . . .

It would surely not, in itself, overcome the intransigence imposed upon us all by selective historical memory and by skewed human thought, but it would point the way—it would be a beginning.

And the way it would point—the beginning it would make—would involve human survival, and that is certainly worth the effort.

Once again, Mars. The most earthlike planet—yet so different and so mysteriously alluring. The truest significance of Mars may be that it represents the Space Age in both substance and symbol. It inspires engineers to dream and dreamers to seek action, and it pulls all of them toward new possibilities that reach beyond the cold war. Policy-makers in our generation must learn to exploit those possibilities.

For a successful transition to a potentially liberating Space Age is by no means certain. The list of extinct species runs much longer than the list of survivors. As the most intelligent species, we seem bent upon earning the distinction of becoming the first to manage our own extinction. Our political intellects are expanding in a narrowing environment. Our failure is of the imagination.

FOUR

THE MOUNTAIN MOVES

13 / SENATE HEARING

Although I was not a member of the Senate Foreign Relations Committee, Senators Mathias and Pell generously invited me to participate in planning for the September 13, 1984, hearing, and to join them in questioning the witnesses. The witness list was crucial. During the two years that I had been trying to bring the space cooperation issue to the attention of the public, members of the media always asked: "When's the hearing?" A congressional hearing legitimized a new issue and gave it dramatic focus. Confrontations between witnesses and congressional inquisitors made news. In our case, though, the hearing format created an unusual media problem. Scientist-witnesses testifying *against* Star Wars insured the courtroom drama that attracted media attention. But our scientist-witnesses would move onto another plane and examine what nations of East and West might do together in space. We thus faced the possibility that the issue would still escape widespread attention because (irony of ironies) cooperation lacked the drama of confrontation. If we were to reach the public and protect the integrity of our message, we needed authoritative and

121

recognizable witnesses who could dramatize the issue without polarizing it.

One of the first persons I contacted was an old friend, James Michener, whose novel *Space* had been part of my education on the subject. We had first met twenty-five years earlier when Michener settled in Honolulu while working on a novel. He asked me to help him learn more about a group of Japanese-Americans, many of them World War II veterans educated on the G.I. Bill of Rights, who won control of Hawaii's territorial legislature in 1954 from an entrenched aristocracy of traders and plantation owners. I was one of that band. Michener assembled a few of us at his home for a discussion that continued nearly till dawn. At the time, I had no idea that we were providing him with information he would use to shape one of the characters in the novel *Hawaii*. Later, in 1964, we both ran for the U.S. House of Representatives—he from Bucks County, Pennsylvania. I won, but, fortunately for millions of readers, James Michener lost his bid for Congress and resumed his career as a novelist. When I initiated my space cooperation effort in 1982, Michener offered his support.

Now, in 1984, he was in Texas at work on another panoramic novel about an American state. I wrote him at his office at the University of Texas in Austin and brought him up to date on my space activities, including the proposal for a long-term Mars program. Might he be willing, I asked, to write a letter that I could introduce into the hearing record? He replied a few days later.

All persons interested in the development of outer space follow with keen attention your attempts to guide its use into constructive channels. For some years now the proper utilization of space has been a major concern of mine, and I constantly hope that ways may be found to bring international order into this vital arena . . .

Manned travel to the planets is now practical. Permanent settlements on the Moon can be established at any time we wish. Low-orbiting space stations are already in existence to a degree and their proliferation is limited only by budget . . .

Senator, I am speaking only of what we can do right now with the inventions we already have in mind. If we project our present rate of development ahead fifty years, only the most imaginative mind would come close to what will be possible . . .

If the speed of invention is so great, I think it incumbent upon us to spend careful thought on what we ought to be doing right now to utilize present capacity and then to pave the way for greater experimentation and achievement later on. That, it seems to me, is the obligation of any major nation.

I am peculiarly involved in such thinking, because I serve on a board whose responsibility it is to combat attempts by the Soviet Union to discolor the truth insofar as international politics are concerned, and I work diligently to protect the reputation of my nation. So I can certainly not be charged with any sentimental favoritism toward the Soviet Union. My job is to monitor her misbehaviors.

But when it comes to the long haul of science and the accomplishments of the future in space, I find myself ardently hoping that the fruitful bi-national cooperation which started with Apollo–Soyuz can be revived, because at some future time, perhaps before the end of this century, such international ventures will be commonplace and we might as well get started correctly now.

I do not see anything contradictory in this recommendation. Of course we are at odds with the Soviet Union on many basic points, and we must protect ourselves, for to do otherwise would be irresponsible or worse. But we must also inhabit the earth with the Russians and share in whatever forward steps are taken. This is a tricky co-responsibility, but I believe the United States is alert enough to manage it . . .

Now as to the specific targets of cooperation, my imagination cannot be as freewheeling as that of scientists who are experts in these fields, but three possibilities dominate my attention: (1) further exploration of the Moon, with the reminder that the Soviets got there first with their cameras and their rovers and thus had the privilege of naming most of the features on the far side; (2) manned exploration of Mars, which would be a major effort requiring enormous planning and much more than a year of absence from the Earth; and (3) extensive further exploration of the solar system, including concentration on problems relating to the Sun, whose power ensures our existence on Earth.

Could the United States conduct these space explorations alone? Yes, but it would be more fruitful, I believe, if we cooperated with the Soviet Union and with other space-competent nations in joint enterprises where scientific enlightenment is the goal. We shall be driven to isolated experimentation in those cases where military competency is at stake, but I do not believe that we should allow that necessity to dominate the world's behavior in space.

I therefore endorse heartily Senate Joint Resolution 236 and pray that it will become a guiding policy statement for our nation.

Next I decided to contact Dr. Arthur C. Clarke, my nomination for Space Age man for all seasons. When he wasn't guiding our imaginations to new celestial worlds, Clarke applied his considerable scientific acumen to translating his visions into practical reality. In a sense, the Space Age began when, shortly after World War II, Arthur Clarke conceptualized the first communications satellite. I had read his essays on the unifying powers of Space Age technology, in which he moved a step beyond Marshall McLuhan's global village and postulated a global family. But I was especially drawn to his most recent novel, *2010: Odyssey Two*, the sequel to his epic *2001: A Space Odyssey*. *2010* told the story of a joint U.S.–U.S.S.R. mission to Jupiter.

Dr. Clarke lived halfway around the world, in the island nation of Sri Lanka, off the coast of India. Through his agent in New York, Russell Galen, I obtained his address. Late one night at the office, as I was writing to Clarke to ask him for a letter of support, I happened to glance over at the television set across from my desk, with its attached video cassette recorder, and it occurred to me: Clarke was a genius at imaginative presentation—why not invite him to submit his testimony on a videotape?

His reply came by telephone from Sri Lanka. He loved the idea. He had his own private filming studio. He would put his other work aside and begin at once.

The Clarke videotape arrived by courier on Monday, September 10, barely three days before the hearing. But the videotape was made on the European PAL system, and I couldn't find a film laboratory in Washington that could convert it to the American system in time for the hearing. When Clarke learned by phone of my difficulty, he activated his own private global communications network. The next thing I knew, the videotape was being rushed to a laboratory in New York, converted, returned to my office the next morning. Never to my knowledge had a witness worked harder, at his own considerable expense, to deliver testimony at a congressional hearing.

I previewed the videotape on Wednesday evening in the Senate recording studio. It ran for fifteen minutes—precisely the length requested—and it was superb. It opened like a movie, with title and credits. I had requested Clarke's views on an international Mars mission, and he replied with:

A MARTIAN ODYSSEY
by Arthur C. Clarke
Chancellor, University of Moratuwa
Fellow of King's College, London
VIDEO PRESENTATION TO
THE COMMITTEE ON FOREIGN RELATIONS,
UNITED STATES SENATE
1984 September 13

125

Arthur Clarke appeared on the screen, seated at a desk in his book-lined study in Sri Lanka, a trim, balding gentleman wearing a gray suit, light blue shirt, and royal-blue tie, relaxed, almost bemused at being called upon to explain what seemed to him so obvious. With a true director's eye, he broke up his lecture by shifting camera angles, occasionally using personal mementos to illustrate a point—a photograph with Soviet cosmonaut Alexei Leonov, an inscribed portrait of American astronaut Tom Stafford.

Clarke left no doubt how he felt about the Soviet regime. Not only had he dedicated *2010* to Leonov and Andrei Sakharov, but the seven Russian crew members in the novel were named after Soviet dissidents. "My Moscow friend and editor failed to spot these curious coincidences," Clarke recounted, "and has accordingly lost his job."

Clarke understood the cold war, and he also understood the stupidity and futility of carrying it into the cosmos. With his usual foresight, he had issued his first warnings against that prospect in the 1940s. Space weapons were incompatible with any creative vision of our future in space. He called them "technological obscenities."

"Let us now talk about technological decency," Clarke said, and he turned to Mars:

Why are [Soviet] cosmonauts making space endurance records with times approaching those required for the Earth–Mars round trip? You don't need that capability for missions this side of the Moon!

Sooner than they imagine, Americans will have to ask themselves: "Do we stand aside, when the Soviet Union heads for Mars? Do we do it alone? Or do we go with them?" . . .

I am not so naïve as to imagine that this could be achieved without excruciating difficulty, and major changes in the present political climate. But those changes *have* to be made . . .

126

Alas, the Foreign Relations Committee never saw Clarke's presentation. I learned at the last minute that committee rules forbade viewing videotaped testimony. There was legitimate concern that too many witnesses might simply send in videotapes, thus avoiding direct questions. When he learned of our problem, Clarke offered to contact INTELSAT and work out a direct satellite hookup to Sri Lanka that would allow committee members to quiz him as much as they liked. But that would have placed too great a strain on the Senate's limited electronic capabilities. As usual, Arthur Clarke was ahead of his time. At least I had the videotape transcript he had wisely provided and could submit it for the hearing record.

But no matter how prominent the witnesses, written testimony wasn't enough. Fortunately, Dr. Carl Sagan responded that he would be happy to testify in person. Sagan, who was one of the first scientists to endorse the space cooperation resolution, had appeared at many other committee hearings as an outspoken critic of Star Wars. For our hearing, I was more interested in the other Carl Sagan whom the Congress didn't know well enough—Cornell University's brilliant cosmologist and key science team member of the Viking missions to Mars, author and narrator of *Cosmos*, the book and television series that inspired a generation of Americans, a scientist who could describe our future in space with down-to-earth authority and a sense of soaring wonder.

With testimony from Arthur Clarke, James Michener, and Carl Sagan, and with a solid report from the OTA scientists' symposium, I felt we were in excellent shape to present a strong case to the Foreign Relations Committee and to the public. We had less than three hours to do it. The hearing convened on September 13 at 10 a.m., and the committee could not extend our time beyond 1 p.m.

First to testify was Dr. Bernard Burke, a prominent MIT astrophysicist who had served as chairman of the OTA scientists' symposium on space cooperation. Burke delivered their report and summarized its findings. The OTA panel, he said, "represented virtually all aspects of space science and all had experience working

127

with Soviet scientists or with data resulting from Soviet space science research." Then, after highlighting a number of possible cooperative ventures, Burke delivered the panel's conclusions:

1. Important scientific interchanges continue today, demonstrating the willingness of U.S. and Soviet scientists to cooperate . . .

2. Soviet capabilities are increasing rapidly in many areas of space science.

3. As Soviet capabilities have increased, their space program has become more open.

4. Increased Soviet mission capabilities mean that a fundamental change has occurred in the relative balance between the U.S. and Soviet space programs. In certain scientific areas, we may now have more to gain from the Soviets than they from us.

"A fundamental change has occurred in the relative balance between U.S. and Soviet space programs." Now, for the first time, the Congress was being told about it by those most competent to testify. And, for a change, we weren't hearing a call for another wasteful space race. These are the facts, Burke said, and the rational response to them would be to resume the gradual progress toward greater East–West space cooperation that we had broken off in 1982, even as other free-world nations were increasing their cooperative activities with the U.S.S.R.

Similar words of advice came from three other scientists who joined Burke at the witness table—Carl Sagan; Harold Masursky of the U.S. Geological Survey, whose experience included lunar-sample exchanges with the Soviets in the 1960s and Venus data exchanges in the 1970s and 1980s; and Louis Friedman, executive director of the Planetary Society, the world's largest space interest group.

A spirited question-and-answer session followed. I had intended to elicit the scientists' views on Mars activities, but Senator Mathias beat me to it when he asked why the Soviets were devoting so much time and effort to long-duration flight. The transcript:

> *Mr. Sagan:* The Soviets have now had continuous human performance in near-earth orbital environments for something like seven months. That is comparable to what it takes to go from earth to Mars in certain interplanetary trajectories . . .
>
> *Senator Mathias:* And what you are saying is that this is demonstrated to be biologically possible?
>
> *Mr. Sagan:* The Soviets have now had humans in zero g for about as long as it would take to send humans to Mars . . .
>
> *Senator Mathias:* I see Dr. Masursky wants to interject.
>
> *Mr. Masursky:* They have said many times that they will send men to Mars, and we cannot think of a reason for keeping men in space for that long otherwise. That is a clear indication of their intention.

With the allotted time running out, I limited my questions exclusively to Mars by asking for further details on Soviet long-duration flight activities,* our own Mars efforts, and the benefits of coordinating already scheduled U.S. and U.S.S.R. scientific missions to Mars near the end of the decade. To provide additional background for our discussion, I also presented the committee with a report I had commissioned from the senior space analyst of the Congressional Research Service, Marcia Smith, reviewing U.S. and Soviet interest in Mars, past missions, and future plans. And, of course, the committee also received the statements of Clarke and Michener endorsing a joint Mars mission.

---

* *Even as I spoke, a record-breaking three-man Soviet crew was beginning its 220th consecutive day, well over seven months, in orbit aboard a Salyut space station. They finally landed on October 2, 1984.*

The Mars emphasis was strategic. The perspective it opened would take time to grasp. I wanted to introduce the idea to Congress early, and in a solid scientific and foreign-policy context, so it would be recognized as a possible *long-term* space objective that responded to the unique character and requirements of the Space Age.

The hearing concluded with testimony from NASA and the State Department. NASA was in a bind. The agency would be responsible for implementing a renewed space agreement. But it lacked the authority to comment on whether it should be renewed. That was a policy question, the responsibility of the State Department. Nonetheless, James Morrison, of NASA's International Affairs Division, praised the fruitfulness of past cooperative activities.

The State Department spokesman, Deputy Assistant Secretary Charles Horner, wandered over the history of U.S.–U.S.S.R. cooperation before coming to the point: "Given the Soviet attitude toward the President's simulated space-rescue proposal, I believe that it would be premature to address the possibility of a new overall space agreement or even project specific agreement between our two governments."

But that didn't make any sense. All other specific U.S.–U.S.S.R. scientific exchange activities had been *preceded* by the signing of an umbrella agreement. We were asking the Soviets to accept a sequence that violated standards governing all U.S.–U.S.S.R. bilateral activities. Obviously, opponents of the space agreement had control of United States policy.

14 / PRESIDENTIAL COMMITMENT

"When's the hearing?"

For two years, we had faced that question from reporters. Now at last they had it, with testimony from Clarke, Michener, and Sagan, plus a landmark OTA panel report. But although a few science journals were represented, no one from the major media showed up, and the American public remained in the dark about our efforts.

I was pleased with the outcome, nonetheless. We had assembled a solid body of evidence that impressed the Foreign Relations Committee, especially Chairman Charles Percy. Working closely with Mathias and Pell, Percy redrafted the resolution to soften space arms-race language that the Administration found unacceptable. The new draft also endorsed the President's space-rescue proposal, which was fine with me so long as it came in a context that recognized the primary need to renew the overall space co-operation agreement. On Monday, October 2, the Foreign Relations Committee unanimously approved Senate Joint Resolution 236 and recommended that it be taken up by the full Senate.

The decision on what legislation reached the Senate floor for a vote was up to the Majority Leader, Howard Baker, and he was besieged. With final adjournment scheduled for that Friday, the chances of our measure being considered in the closing crush of business seemed all but impossible. Besides, even if it passed the Senate, there was still the House, where Representative Levine's companion measure remained bottled up in committee. Then Baker decided to extend the session into the following week.

On October 9, we obtained Baker's consent to place Senate Joint Resolution 236 on the calendar under a unanimous-consent agreement. If a single Senator objected, the measure could be blocked from discussion. No one objected, and suddenly I was standing at my desk on the Senate floor summarizing a two-year effort and concluding: "If we want a vision of the future worth pursuing, this is it. If we want small steps that will set us moving toward it, we have them. The stage is set. All we need is the courage to do what political leaders are supposed to do: Act!" The Senate acted and passed the joint resolution unanimously.

Over in the House, Levine had wasted no time. Pointing to the Senate Foreign Relations Committee's favorable action, he asked House Foreign Affairs Committee chairman Dante Fascell to negotiate rapid release of a version identical to ours, for consideration on the floor under a unanimous-consent agreement. But a couple of committee members apparently opposed the clause requiring that the President submit a progress report on his efforts by March 1, 1985. Levine had no choice but to delete the disputed clause, whereupon the measure was sent to the House floor, where it passed without opposition.

Still, although both versions had passed, their language had to be made identical before Senate Joint Resolution 236 could be forwarded to the President for signing. Late in the evening of October 12, only a few hours before adjournment of the 98th Congress, Howard Baker answered my appeal to act on an amended Senate version that eliminated the clause the House had dropped.

The amended Senate version passed. The next day, a unanimously approved joint resolution was delivered to the White House for the President's signature.

The last-second passage of the space cooperation resolution took the Administration by surprise and posed a dilemma. When a resolution or bill reached the President's desk after Congress's adjournment, he had ten working days (excluding weekends and holidays) to sign it. If he failed to act, the measure died by "pocket veto." That was the recommendation of a few hardliners. But in his campaign for reelection the President had come out for better relations with the Soviets and the Presidential election was only a few days away. The day before the pocket-veto deadline, which was seven days before the election, we finally made news. *The New York Times* reported that President Reagan was deciding whether to veto a congressional resolution calling for renewed U.S.–U.S.S.R. cooperation in space. I couldn't have asked for better timing.

Late in the afternoon on deadline day, the President signed Senate Joint Resolution 236. In an accompanying statement, he first reiterated his commitment to space exploration and cooperation in general, then turned to the resolution: "I find portions of the language contained in the preamble to the Joint Resolution very speculative. However, I have stated several times our desire to increase contacts with the Soviets on cooperation in space programs which are mutually beneficial and productive. As part of this effort, the United States has offered to carry out with the Soviet Union a joint simulated space rescue mission. We believe this and similar cooperative programs offer practical benefits for all mankind. It is in that spirit that I today sign this Joint Resolution."

Upon hearing the news, I quickly drafted a statement applauding the President's decision. I had always been convinced that President Reagan favored the concept I was trying to advance. It was completely in tune with his own forward-looking inclinations.

The challenge was to bring it to his attention. There are so many competing constituencies within government, and so many competing issues, that the process of bringing an idea before the President that isn't pushed by an influential interest group or isn't a response to an immediate crisis requires a major effort against long odds.

Everyone seemed stunned—pleasantly or otherwise—by the joint resolution's passage into law. The scientists who had lent their support couldn't get over the outcome. ("Frankly, Senator, none of us really believed that your resolution would pass," Dave Morrison confided.) Our two-year campaign had carried the space cooperation issue from obscurity into the legislative and executive councils of government. It had made cooperation a topic of open discussion and debate. Even behind the scenes, it had encouraged reevaluation and the staking out of positions pro and con. Until then, the cons had controlled the atmosphere.

Moreover, we had laid a foundation for the issue's eventual consideration by the public at large in the context it deserved. We had a public law, an impressive hearing record, a growing number of endorsements building on a solid scientific base. All in a context that looked beyond the closed loop of insanity of the cold war.

It kept coming back to what my father had taught me.

15 / THE MARS RESOLUTION

January 21, 1985

I closed the door and glanced at the clock on my desk. Nearly 4 p.m. For the first time since arriving at the Capitol that morning for the President's inauguration, I was alone. In a few minutes, the Senate would convene briefly, perhaps for an hour, to mark the opening of the 99th Congress. I reached into my briefcase for the Mars resolution and its accompanying floor statement and began revising them yet again. Even in this preliminary form, the proposal would have to be guided into the political arena with great care.

I slipped the resolution into a manila envelope and departed quickly for the subway connecting the Senate office building with the Capitol.

Not surprisingly, considering the many Inauguration Day activities everywhere else, the Senate Chamber was nearly deserted. Alan Simpson of Wyoming, the Republican Whip, stood in for the absent Majority Leader, Bob Dole. Slade Gorton of Washington did the same for the Vice-President, whom the Constitution des-

135

ignated President of the Senate. No other Republicans were in evidence. On the Democratic side of the aisle, I spotted only a few newly elected Senators who had dropped by to inspect the premises—Jay Rockefeller of West Virginia, John Kerry of Massachusetts, and Paul Simon of Illinois, the latter a friend and former colleague of mine in the House who had defeated Chuck Percy in a tight campaign. A scant two dozen spectators were in the balcony gallery that looked down on the Senate floor from four sides. I went to my desk and asked to be heard. According to practice, a Senate stenographer moved up the aisle and took a position opposite me, his stenograph machine held horizontally at his waist by a shoulder strap. As I began to speak, his fingers nimbly recorded my words for the *Congressional Record*:

Mr. President, I rise to introduce a resolution pertaining to a distant planet that has fascinated the human species since our earliest ancestors first contemplated the heavens—Mars.

Some of my colleagues may wonder: Has the Senator from Hawaii lost his senses? Here the United States Senate convenes to address a veritable avalanche of pressing issues . . . and the Senator from Hawaii talks about Mars?

But, Mr. President, I believe we also have a duty to try to see beyond the cascading issues that engulf us daily, even while we are considering them. No one likes to be called a reactionary, but if we simply react to problems as they occur, what else are we? Too often, it seems, harried policy-makers only have time to consider the future when it has nothing to offer because the encroaching present has already violated its potential.

I do not accept that, Mr. President. I do not believe the American people sent us here only to respond to their immediate needs. I believe our constituents also hope that someday, perhaps, we will respond to their aspirations as well, and not merely by concluding our speeches with misty visions borrowed from greeting cards or uplifting quotes from folklore. The future is neither nostalgia nor a dream but an unfolding concrete reality, filled with promise, meant to be acted upon pragmatically now, with intelligence and imagination, by those of us who are entrusted with the responsibilities of government.

As the preambular clauses in my resolution indicate, the prospect of another costly and wasteful space race with the Russians is anything but science fiction. At a Senate Foreign Relations Committee hearing last September 13, a panel of U.S. space scientists testified unanimously that the Russians were going to Mars, perhaps as early as the 1990s. Are we setting ourselves up for another Sputnik? Many experts believe so.

We can, of course, wait characteristically until the last minute, then launch a crash program to beat the Soviets to Mars, at stupendous cost. And after that, Neptune? Pluto? The next galaxy? Even in the context of our self-perpetuating "real world," we cannot anticipate racing the Soviets into a cosmic infinity.

As the Space Age unfolds, it is generating new realities and new opportunities unlike any heretofore imaginable. Cosmic is no metaphor out there. Only fantasists talk about riding through space, planting flags, and defending trade routes with rocket ships. Realists recognize that the sheer immensity of space generates requirements for survival that, ultimately, will force the superpowers to cooperate. At a certain point, anything other than international exploration of the cosmos from our tiny planet will cease to make any sense at all. In our intense absorption with events of the moment, we have failed to recognize how close to that point we really are.

But before we can reach it, we must develop policies that respond to the unfolding realities of the Space Age, that move out to meet it on its own uniquely promising terms. Without such policies, earthbound civilization can only wind up recoiling upon itself. It is not often remarked, Mr. President, that the space-weapons systems currently under development will reach scarcely above the atmosphere. Regardless of their merits, those systems are irrelevant to the challenge of space exploration. For that compelling reason alone, it is in our interest to develop a separate track for international space exploration, even as we negotiate with the Soviets at Geneva and strengthen our defenses at home. It would permit us to test a new context far more promising than the one which currently prevails. As it happens, the planet Mars offers an initial guiding step in that direction.

Toward the end of this decade, an unusual convergence in space exploration will occur. In 1988, the U.S.S.R. will launch an unmanned scientific mission to the Mars moon Phobos. In 1990, the United States will launch its Mars Geochemical / Climatology Orbiter.* It makes no sense not to coordinate the two scheduled missions, so as to insure maximum scientific return. But, due to long lead times for such activities, meaningful cooperation cannot be achieved unless action is taken within the next few months. My resolution proposes that the President direct the administrator of NASA to explore the opportunities for coordinating the two Mars missions while there is still time, in the context of the Administration's committed effort to renew the U.S.–U.S.S.R. space cooperation agreement in accordance with legislation the President signed last October 30 . . .

Coordinating the 1988 and 1990 Mars missions—which would require no technology transfer on either side—represents an opportunity that deserves the highest priority. Among other things, it could open the way to a wider range of cooperative activities in other areas of space science, such as solar-terrestrial physics, astrophysics, and plasma physics. And, of course, it would set the stage for further collaboration in the exploration of Mars.

With the preceding in mind, my resolution also proposes that NASA prepare a report examining the opportunities for joint East–West Mars-related activities, including an un-

Our spacecraft was later renamed Mars Observer.

manned sample return and all other activities that might contribute to an international manned mission to Mars, perhaps at the turn of the century. I should point out that Mars contingency planning is nothing new at NASA . . . Designs for Mars missions have been percolating on NASA's back burners for twenty-five years. I understand that even now NASA may be gearing up for yet another manned Mars mission study, in keeping with the President's admirable intention to establish goals beyond the space station that "will carry us well into the next century." In effect, my resolution suggests that such a study also encompass the possibilities for international cooperation, so we can at least consider that option alongside the alternative of an absurdly wasteful U.S.–U.S.S.R. race to Mars, while we still have a choice.

In sum, Mr. President, my resolution does two things. On the one hand, it urges policy-makers to exploit an immediate opportunity for space cooperation. On the other hand, it casts that opportunity in the context of requirements generated by an almost unimaginably expansive new age which promises to render many aspects of current thought and action obsolete, if we manage to keep human civilization intact long enough to enter it. I hope we will devote greater consideration to devising ways to take advantage of those uniquely promising opportunities on the horizon, even as we now stand on the brink. If successful, we will earn the gratitude of future generations—indeed, of whole new worlds.

As I was concluding my remarks, Senator William Proxmire of Wisconsin emerged from the cloakroom where floor proceedings were piped in. He took his seat two desks away, an intent expression on his face. Bill Proxmire, of all people. He had been the most outspoken critic of the Apollo–Soyuz project. Proxmire, the Senate's most assiduous and effective critic of wasteful spending, had called Apollo–Soyuz a "$250 million handshake." Would he automatically perceive my proposal in the same light, or would he recognize that it represented something new? The Senate steno-grapher recorded the exchange immediately following the conclusion of my statement.

> *Mr. Proxmire:* Mr. President, will the distinguished Senator from Hawaii yield?
> *Mr. Matsunaga:* Mr. President, I am happy to yield to the distinguished Senator from Wisconsin.
> *Mr. Proxmire:* First, Mr. President, I ask permission of the Senator from Hawaii to be co-sponsor of this resolution.
> *Mr. Matsunaga:* I am happy to have the Senator join.
> *Presiding Officer:* Without objection, it is so ordered.
> *Mr. Proxmire:* Mr. President, I want to congratulate the Senator from Hawaii on this resolution, an excellent resolution . . .

What a relief! I had immense respect for Bill Proxmire. He was a man of integrity and commitment. When he said something, he meant it, a hundred percent. He had listened and he had decided, without prejudice, on the merits of the proposal. Moments later, Paul Simon of Illinois walked up and asked to be listed as a co-sponsor as well. I wrote their names in at the top of the resolution, went over the text one last time, then delivered it to the Senate Parliamentarian seated at a table in the front of the Chamber. Al Simpson asked if I would mind joining him in concluding the day's business. He moved to recess, I seconded his motion, and, at 5 p.m., there being no objections, Acting President pro tempore Gorton ruled that the inaugural meeting of the United States Senate, 99th Congress, stood in recess until the following day.

I wasn't sure why I had been so determined to introduce the Mars resolution on Inauguration Day. It somehow seemed appropriate. Perhaps it hinted at an inauguration of another kind. Anyhow, it was done.

Although I was delighted to have Proxmire and Simon on board, their engagement as original co-sponsors created a serious problem. Suddenly I had a heavily Democratic resolution. That wasn't how I wanted to introduce a theme that transcended partisan politics. So I took the Mars resolution underground, quickly obtained four Republican co-sponsors, added Clai Pell on the Democratic side, and reintroduced it two weeks later as a bipartisan measure. Leading the list of Republican co-introducers was Slade Gorton of Washington, who had presided in the Senate the day the Mars resolution was introduced, the judicious and knowledgeable chairman of the Space Subcommittee of the Commerce Committee that authorized funds for NASA. Gorton was joined by Republicans Nancy Kassebaum of Kansas, Robert Stafford of Vermont, and stellar "Mac" Mathias. They were matched by Proxmire, Simon, Pell, and me, for a balanced lineup of four Democrats and four Republicans.

Although the resolution's requirements were extremely modest, its opening words pointed toward a limitless future. I was trying to remind policy-makers that, in addition to the self-perpetuating requirements of the closed loop of insanity which absorbed their single-minded attention, there was a new age to deal with. We had broken off the space agreement in 1982 because of Poland. Now, when we were considering its renewal, might we perhaps also consider the long-term significance of space?

Would someone in the policy-making councils of government please look *up*?

16 / THE ISY

I was convinced that Americans who wanted our country to proceed rapidly with space weapons did so from the sincere conviction that we had no choice. Such were the rules of the cold war. The real challenge was to create a choice that, in slow but persistently advancing stages, explored Space Age opportunities that reached beyond the cold war.

How to do so was my principal concern during the early months of 1985. My Mars resolution called on NASA to prepare a report examining ways in which future Mars-related activities might be coordinated. To be on the safe side, I proposed to Slade Gorton, chairman of the Senate's Space Subcommittee, that the overall NASA authorization bill also include a requirement for a report on coordinating future Mars efforts. In that way, even if Congress failed to pass my resolution, one of its main objectives would still be implemented. Gorton, who was the Mars resolution's chief co-sponsor, readily agreed. At about the same time, in an article requested by the Planetary Society for its periodical, *The Planetary Report*, I proposed that an East–West Mars working group be established to coordinate activities in the 1990s and beyond. Reports, working groups—these were initial ways to start people thinking about a transition to the long-term.

But they obviously weren't enough. The time between possible renewal of the U.S.–U.S.S.R. space cooperation agreement in the 1980s and eventual exploration and settlement of Mars during the next generation was still too great and the concept of "building blocks" to Mars still too limited in its short-term application. The Mars project also needed broad-based intermediary objectives that would immediately mobilize governments and the world public and set the stage for Mars.

Early in 1985, the American Institute of Aeronautics and Astronautics, or AIAA, and the Planetary Society decided to co-sponsor a conference in Washington, D.C., on human exploration of Mars. They scheduled it for July 20, the anniversary of the first human landing on the moon by astronauts Neil Armstrong and Buzz Aldrin in 1969. In response to an invitation to participate, I wrote the president of the AIAA, John McLucas, and the president of the Planetary Society, Carl Sagan, with a suggestion. Why not move up the date by three days, to July 17, and commemorate the tenth anniversary of Apollo–Soyuz; and why not invite the astronauts and cosmonauts who had participated in that event?

My suggestions were adopted. America's Apollo–Soyuz astronauts—Tom Stafford, Deke Slayton, and Vance Brand—were delighted at the prospect of a reunion. A cable was dispatched to Vladimir Kotelnikov, first vice-president of the Soviet Academy of Sciences and overall director of Soviet cooperative activities in manned space flight, inviting Soviet cosmonauts Alexei Leonov and Valery Kubasov. How Kotelnikov would respond was anybody's guess. If the Soviet government agreed to send the Apollo–Soyuz cosmonauts, national attention for the Mars exploration theme would be assured.

That exciting prospect was in the back of my mind when, in late April, I received a visit from Professor John Simpson of the

University of Chicago. Simpson had designed instruments for a Pioneer 10 spacecraft launched in 1972 that, eleven years later, in 1983, passed beyond Neptune and Pluto to become the first man-made object to leave the solar system. As we talked in my Washington office, Pioneer 10 was three billion miles away and heading toward a rendezvous with galactic space around 1990. Amazingly, Simpson's instruments were still sending back data.

Simpson had come to talk to me about another mission launched in December 1984—the twin spacecraft Soviet Vega mission to Halley's comet. About a year and a half before that launching, Simpson's team at the University of Chicago developed an instrument for collecting dust from comets which was superior to anything in use. Since the United States had declined to join the Halley space fleet, Simpson offered his instrument to the West European entry. But the European mission was already booked. Roald Sagdeev of the Soviet Union learned of those discussions through the international grapevine and offered Simpson a place on the Soviet spacecraft. The only hitch was that the United States had canceled its space cooperation agreement with the Soviets. Simpson and Sagdeev put their heads together, brought in their West German colleagues, and came up with an elaborate procedure to "denationalize" Simpson's experiment by making it part of a West German contribution to the Soviet Vega mission.

With that hurdle overcome, Simpson went to the State Department. To his good fortune, the Under-Secretary of State at the time was Kenneth Dam, a former provost of the University of Chicago. Dam guided Simpson through the bureaucracy. To overcome suspicions about technology transfer, Simpson "back-designed" his instrument, so that it relied on ten-year-old technology, and he prepared a description of each component, down to the simplest nuts and bolts. After numerous letters, meetings, and briefings, he was finally given the green light. "Compared to its politics, the science of this mission was easy," Simpson said. "Isn't there any way to be more rational about this?"

At that point in our discussion, Simpson wistfully recalled the atmosphere of the 1957–58 International Geophysical Year. He had served as one of twelve members of the international organizing committee for the IGY. He told me it had been the most satisfying experience of his professional life. "And, Senator," he said, "it was inspiringly successful even in the teeth of the cold war."

Well, not quite. Sputnik had overshadowed much of the IGY's impact in the public mind. But at the working level, Simpson was right. The global achievements of the IGY have never been matched.

During the next few days, my reflections kept coming back to the IGY. Why not do it again? But how? When? The 1957 IGY had been the third in a sequence. First came the Polar Year in 1882; then the Second Polar Year in 1932, fifty years later; then the decision to cut the interval to twenty-five years, in response to rapid advances in science, and to make its coverage global, which led to the IGY in 1957. According to that schedule, we should have had another IGY in 1982. I contacted the National Academy of Sciences. It turned out that a delayed sequel was under consideration, through the International Council of Scientific Unions, to be called the International Geosphere / Biosphere Program, or IGBP. It would begin around 1990 and perhaps continue beyond 2000. Its theme would be "global habitability"—managing our environment on a global scale. The space component of the IGBP would consist of "earth-looking" satellites conducting meteorological and geophysical measurements of our planet. But this 1990s sequel to the International Geophysical Year, the IGY that launched the Space Age, would not explore space. Then the idea hit me.

An International Space Year. An ISY. I pulled out Arthur Clarke's testimony at the previous September's hearing: "Is it absurdly optimistic to hope that, by Columbus Day 1992, the United States and the Soviet Union will have emerged from their long winter of sterile confrontation?" Clarke had in mind, of course, the five hundredth anniversary of the discovery of America. And I recalled Carl Sagan having warned that the Soviets might be planning a major manned mission in space in 1992, perhaps even to the vicinity of Mars, to mark the seventy-fifth anniversary of the Russian Revolution of 1917.

An ISY in 1992 fit our national interest and it fit the expansive interests of the Space Age. Since it would involve many nations, U.S.-U.S.S.R. cooperation might be tested in a broader and less volatile atmosphere than in a head-to-head encounter. Since the other two most developed space powers, Western Europe and Japan, were our allies, we would have the Soviets outnumbered on major issues in case they tried any propaganda ploys. As for the Soviets, they would find it difficult to reject participation in an International Space Year when they were seeking to increase international participation in their own space activities. The timing for preliminary discussions was just right. Planning for the IGY began in 1950, seven years in advance of the event. We were seven years from 1992.

Coming forward with the proposal now could also alert the American people to the risk of a major Soviet propaganda triumph in 1992. Besides being the seventy-fifth anniversary of the Russian Revolution, 1992 was also the thirty-fifth anniversary of Sputnik, which was launched during the IGY. It would be in character for the Soviets to plan another Sputnik surprise for 1992, but on a grander scale—perhaps a manned interplanetary mission, or at least the launching of a multi-pod space station well in advance of our own space station, which was scheduled for 1993 or later. Meanwhile, we would be commemorating the discovery of America with ceremonies featuring replicas of the *Niña*, the *Pinta*, and the *Santa María* and actors in fifteenth-century costumes. The contrast would be embarrassing to the extreme. Even if we recognized the danger by, say, 1989, it would be too late. We needed *lead time*.

Moreover, that seven-year lead time was just about right for encouraging far-seeing Space Age perceptions without the target seeming too remote. An ISY would serve as an intermediate stage between renewal of the U.S.–U.S.S.R. space agreement and consideration of large-scale missions near the turn of the century. It could develop as a test of cooperation. If it proved successful, we could move on to bigger things.

Finally, the concept was sufficiently broad to encourage contributions at every level. Schools could become involved, from grade schools to universities, and public service groups, institutes, professional societies. Preparation could proceed like a sustained space-launch countdown. As 1992 approached, the circle of interest would grow and anticipation would heighten. An ISY in 1992 would generate broad-based, sustained interest in space activities of a sort never yet attained, pointing toward a concrete target with which everyone could identify.

Yes, everyone. That was what I liked best about it. Here finally was an activity that moved beyond the opposites. Who was the ISY against? No one. Who was it for? Everyone. Arms control? Star Wars? If they interest you, pursue them. But here's something else. It's big—so big it takes your breath away.

But how does one start an International Space Year? The IGY had been organized by the scientific community through the International Council of Scientific Unions. The IGBP was following the same route. An ISY, however, would be distinctive in the size and scope of its highlighting activities. Its program would require active high-level participation by national governments. Unlike the IGBP, starting an ISY would require major political initiatives.

I drafted a Senate Joint Resolution containing two requirements. First, it invited the President to discuss an ISY with foreign leaders. Second, it directed NASA, in association with the State Department, the National Academy of Sciences, the National Science Foundation, and other relevant public and private agencies, to explore the opportunities for an ISY in 1992 and report its findings to Congress in the spring of 1986. The report would give substance to the idea and provide a basis for further discussions, legislation, hearings, and other activities that would move an ISY onto the international political agenda.

I was particularly anxious to see NASA play a leading role. Our space agency was, in a sense, a child of the IGY. It was created in 1958, in the aftermath of Sputnik, and it had been involved in one space race after another ever since. An ISY would permit NASA to reestablish itself in a less desperate and more forward-looking context.

The date of the resolution's introduction was determined by the upcoming Mars conference. Early in June, the Russians responded favorably to the invitation to send their two Apollo–Soyuz cosmonauts, thus insuring national prominence for the event. When it turned out that the Smithsonian Air and Space Museum was already scheduling an international cooperation conference on July 17, the AIAA and the Planetary Society moved theirs up to July 16. That meant I could announce the resolution at the Mars conference on July 16, and introduce it in the Senate on July 17, the tenth anniversary of the Apollo–Soyuz docking—with, I hoped, the reunited Apollo–Soyuz crew in the Senate gallery.

The Mars conference speech was a pleasure to draft. At last, I wasn't arguing against anything and could even point out the ironic humor in our space relationship with the Soviets. I noted how U.S. space proponents had always relied heavily on the Soviets by invoking that perennial winning theme: if we don't do it, the Soviets will. "In that important sense," I wrote, "the U.S. and the U.S.S.R. have engaged in a broad program of covert space cooperation for more than a generation. One of its greatest achievements was the Apollo moon project, which was conceived and implemented wholly with the Soviets in mind." Upon learning that Spain already planned to commemorate the five hundredth anniversary of the discovery of America by launching a Hispanic communications satellite in 1992, I put that in the speech and added: "So, if working with the Russians on an ISY leaves anyone with an empty feeling, remember that we can still have a space race with the Spanish."

In researching the speech, I found a surprisingly large number of national space missions already under consideration for the early 1990s which might be coordinated to increase their scientific return, without any risk of technology transfer. It seemed as if the exploration programs of the major space powers were advancing toward a point where not cooperating would become patently absurd. All that was needed to bring them together was a catalyst. I listed five possibilities, although there were many more:

1. *Lunar mission.* The U.S., the U.S.S.R., and Japan are planning scientific missions to the moon within the next decade. Why not coordinate objectives and triple the return?

2. *Comet sample return*—a top priority of U.S. scientists which has been put on the back burner due to limited funds. The U.S., the U.S.S.R., Europe, and Japan are already working closely on a multiple-spacecraft rendezvous with Halley's comet in 1986. Why not follow up with a coordinated mission that would cut costs and bring back the first sample from a comet nucleus?

3. *Project Space Watch.* This is a favorite of mine because it opens out in so many directions. The initial objective, already being pursued by the U.S., is to catalogue all asteroids that might collide with Earth, as a first step toward diverting any of them headed our way. Many scientists believe that a giant asteroid obliterated the dinosaurs sixty-five million years ago. We know that a smaller projectile struck a remote corner of Siberia in 1908 with the force of a 12-megaton hydrogen bomb—a thousand times the power of the weapon that destroyed Hiroshima. A fractional shift in direction and that asteroid might have devastated Moscow, New York, or Los Angeles.

If averting catastrophe isn't enough motivation, there is also the composition of asteroids. They're the most mineral-rich space objects within reach—orbiting bonanzas of iron, nickel, copper, tin, and platinum. While diverting them, we can also exploit them. An initial cataloguing process leads naturally to unmanned reconnaissance missions, culminating eventually in space mining and manufacturing. Already, the Soviets and the French are jointly planning a twin spacecraft mission to Venus that will continue on to two asteroids, flying by one and landing on the other. The launch year is 1991. Instead of watching from the bleachers, why not join them?

4. *VLBI.* The Americans, the Russians, and Europe are in various stages of considering satellites with antennae that would vastly extend the reach of a worldwide network of ground-based radio telescopes—it's called very-long-baseline interferometry, or VLBI. The Soviets are now talking to Europe about a possible 1991 launch. Why not involve everyone in 1992?

5. *Space-station coordination.* In Antarctica, according to principles established during the IGY, the scientific outposts of fourteen nations are in communication with one another and prepared to provide emergency assistance. If space is supposed to represent an advance of civilization, we should at least permit the same for our first orbiting scientific outposts—both of which are due to be constructed in the early 1990s. Space stations should be designed so they can communicate with each other and their crews can aid one another in emergencies. Then I wrote: "The Space Age got off on the wrong foot in 1957, and 1992 offers a unique opportunity to achieve a badly needed correction. This time, we might say to the Soviets: '1992? No Sputniks. No surprises. Let's not confuse our politicians and provoke national frenzies. This time, let's do it right. Let's coordinate in advance and involve as many other nations as we possibly can.' "

I did not include an international manned Mars mission on the ISY list because that would be expecting too much too soon. But I suggested that all long-range planning for Mars missions should include the possibility of joint activity, in the spirit of the ISY. Perhaps, by 1992, the governmental relationships and public interest and enthusiasm generated by the ISY will permit nations to work together toward Mars with an ease that is inconceivable now.

The all-day Mars conference in Washington was a splendid success, thanks to its AIAA and Planetary Society organizers. More than five hundred attendees overflowed the auditorium at the National Academy of Sciences, across the street from the Lincoln

Memorial. In the morning, there were sessions on mission design, required technology for manned Mars flight, biomedical and physiological aspects of sending humans to Mars, and other aspects of a manned Mars mission which demonstrated beyond doubt its technical feasibility. During the lunch break, the Apollo–Soyuz astronauts and cosmonauts held a press conference, and afterward they participated in a ceremony highlighted by the presentation of awards for international cooperation in space. The conference concluded with a lively and enlightening panel discussion on human exploration of Mars, featuring Planetary Society president Carl Sagan, vice-president Bruce Murray, NASA administrator James Beggs, former U.S. senator and astronaut Harrison Schmitt, astronaut Sally Ride, and Roger Bonnet, director of Space Sciences for the European Space Agency.

My speech was delivered at the conclusion of the morning's activities, and I was delighted with its reception. The title was "A Thirty-Year Mars Program—Would the U.S. Congress Support It?" In effect, I answered no—unless steps were first taken to expand public understanding of the significance and potential of space exploration. Hence the need for an ISY.

The next day I was host to the Apollo–Soyuz astronauts for lunch at the Senate dining room. On my left sat retired Air Force Lieutenant General Tom Stafford, who commanded the Apollo craft; on my right, Major General Alexei Leonov, who commanded Soyuz. They were joined by Deke Slayton and Vance Brand of Apollo and Valery Kubasov of Soyuz. I was struck by their camaraderie and the particular closeness between Stafford and Leonov— two commanders who had fought the battle of space together. They told me how they had conducted joint training exercises at Star City, the Soviet space center outside Moscow, and at the Johnson Center in Houston. They had been hoping for a reunion and were overjoyed that, for once, the politicians of their respective nations had cooperated to make it possible. How I wished it could happen more often.

After lunch, I escorted my distinguished guests to the Senate gallery, where the Russians had a firsthand look at American parliamentary procedure. A filibuster was in progress on legislation that would give the President the right to veto individual clauses in an appropriations bill—called a line-item veto. There would be no difficulty interrupting the debate briefly to introduce my ISY resolution. But I also wanted to invite the Apollo–Soyuz crew onto the Senate floor and introduce them to my colleagues, a common practice with visiting dignitaries. That wasn't so easy in the midst of a filibuster. It would require a recess, which, according to parliamentary rules, could close off the filibuster. Democratic leader Robert Byrd and I consulted the parliamentary rule book, the Senate parliamentarian, the Republican leadership, the debaters, and after intense negotiations in full view of our Russian visitors, we finally worked out an arrangement whereby, after my floor statement, the Apollo–Soyuz crew would descend to a Senate reception room, just off the Senate floor, where my colleagues could slip out to meet them.

By a neat coincidence, the docking of Apollo–Soyuz had occurred at 2:17 p.m. Eastern Standard Time on July 17, 1975, ten years almost to the hour of my floor statement. I recalled the words of Valery Kubasov on that day, when he conducted a tour of Soyuz that was broadcast live over American television (Vance Brand did the same aboard Apollo for Russian viewers). As Kubasov was describing the interior of Soyuz, the linked spaceships passed over the Soviet Union. "It would be wrong to ask which country's more beautiful," Kubasov told American viewers. "It could be right to say there is nothing more beautiful than our blue planet." I also described how the Apollo–Soyuz crew had collaborated on an educational film that was shown in thousands of science classrooms in both nations. Could anyone doubt that, if only for a brief moment in history, these brave men had transcended the differences that were sending their nations on a race toward Armageddon?

Then, before submitting the ISY resolution, I told my colleagues: "The unity of planet Earth so evident from space is undermined daily by human conflict, but it survives in our aspirations. The lingering memory of Apollo–Soyuz demonstrates its persistency and hints at an awaiting fulfillment. It probably won't happen in our lifetime. But what has proved impossible on Earth will, I am convinced, eventually prove necessary and unavoidable if humanity is to realize its destiny in the cosmic immensity of the heavens. Meanwhile, governments have an obligation to respond to the deepest aspirations of their citizens in ways that do not conflict with national interest." I was still trying to emphasize, as I always had, that the new frontier of space offered an opportunity for adversaries to discover common goals and build new relationships; that a policy of space cooperation, if pursued with intelligence and imagination, could serve our national interest and the cause of peace and freedom at least as much as the construction of thermonuclear bombs, and it offered considerably more hope for the future.

On July 26, I reintroduced the ISY resolution with Republican Senator Jake Garn, the first member of Congress to fly in space while holding office, as its co-sponsor. To avoid intrusiveness, we deleted a reference to the November summit in Geneva, although the suggestion that the President discuss the ISY with foreign leaders was retained. On that same day, Congressmen Bill Nelson and Robert Walker, chairman and ranking Republican on the House Science and Technology Committee's Space Subcommittee, introduced a companion measure in the House of Representatives.

On November 14, the Senate Foreign Relations Committee unanimously approved our ISY resolution, with minor amendments ably prepared under the direction of the committee chairman, Richard G. Lugar of Indiana. On November 21, the resolution was unanimously passed by the full Senate. On that same day, the Senate and the House also passed a NASA authorization bill that incorporated all of our resolution's objectives, thanks to the support of sympathetic Senate and House conferees. In the bipartisan spirit of the Space Age, the effort for an International Space Year was underway.

FIVE

A SPACE POLICY FOR
THE SPACE AGE

Open opportunity—open government—open competition—open communication. I don't think Americans fully realize the decisive role that openness has played in the formation of our values and our institutions. Other nations have embraced democracy and capitalism, but none with the same unified commitment to openness as the United States. From that commitment comes the unique dynamism—the mobility, flexibility, individual freedom—of American society. Democratic openness is our greatest strength. Our weakness is a failure to fashion intelligent foreign policies that use it.

Pursuit of the cold war is becoming, for lack of an alternative, the American dream. We need the Space Age to rediscover the best in ourselves. It presents America's leaders with an extraordinary opportunity to develop policies that use democratic openness as a force for constructive change. Sustained pursuit of those policies will, in turn, revive and rejuvenate the deepest hopes and aspirations of the American people. In its awesome vastness and grandeur, its transcendent opportunities, the Space Age *is* the American dream, cast onto a cosmic frontier.

Even while dealing with the bitter realities of the cold war, the United States should pursue distinctive Space Age policies whose objective is to go beyond the cold war. That task will place a special burden on the current generation of American leaders, forcing them to live in two worlds at once—a cold war on earth and a new age in space—until the transition from the first to the second is completed. Here are a few suggestions for managing that transition.

17 / THE POLICY CONTEXT

Under current U.S. policies, East–West cooperative activities of every kind—from exchanging dance troupes and symphony orchestras to cooperation in outer space—are lumped in one basket. Our level of involvement in those activities is determined by the overall state of East–West relations. If there is progress in arms control, if Soviet behavior in Africa, the Middle East, and Eastern Europe meets with our approval, then cooperation is possible. But if, after cooperation is established, the Soviet Union behaves disagreeably—martial law is declared in Poland, a further crackdown on dissidents—then the United States indiscriminately scales down or breaks off cooperative programs across the board.

To the extent that it affects space activities, that policy must be revised, for a number of reasons. First and foremost, space belongs in a policy category that recognizes its transcendent scope and significance. The challenge of space is *big*. Cosmic is no metaphor. Distances are measured in millions of miles, missions take years and decades from conception to execution, time zones as we understand them no longer apply. Space is also *new*. The opportunities it offers cannot be perceived, much less exploited, by trying to make the heavens submit to balance-of-power rules and procedures established at the Congress of Vienna in 1815 to govern relations between tiny earthbound nation-states. Space demands new perspectives from policy-makers.

Other nations are recognizing space exploration's unique requirements for coordinated action to meet a superordinate challenge. The nations of Western Europe are jointly producing a rocket (Ariane), a space laboratory (Spacelab), a space platform (Columbus), an integrated Halley's comet mission (Giotto), and are working together on numerous other complex space projects. The tightly integrated activity that Western European nations have sought in vain in the European Common Market has been attained in the European Space Agency in recognition of the new realities of the Space Age. Now the space explorers of Western Europe are moving toward Eastern Europe and the Soviet Union in the same spirit. Eleven nations, including West Germany, France, Sweden, Great Britain, and Ireland, will participate in the Soviets' unmanned scientific mission to the Mars moon Phobos in 1988, and other coordinated activities are in the works. The Europeans are cooperating more with us, to be sure, but the trend on their side is also toward expanded cooperation with the East as the space programs of East and West grow more sophisticated, costly, and complementary in their objectives.

The Soviet Phobos mission is a decade-long undertaking. Under current U.S. policy, even if we were on board at the beginning, our scientists would probably have been required to drop out three or four times along the way, as our policy-makers fired off one "signal" after another at the Soviets to indicate U.S. displeasure with Soviet behavior. But that sort of U.S. behavior would quickly alienate us from everyone involved, including our allies. Whether we like it or not, space cooperation is becoming more international and governments are insulating it from short-term policy shifts in order to pursue its unique long-term potential.

The United States bears a special responsibility not merely to follow but to lead in the move toward greater and enduring cooperation in space. Open cooperation will foster democracy on the space frontier; secrecy and confrontation will foster its totalitarian opposite, regardless of the earthbound ideologies of those involved. *The nature of government in space will depend on the nature of the relationships established while exploring space.*

18 / U.S.–U.S.S.R. RELATIONS IN SPACE

Perhaps the most shallow argument against U.S.–U.S.S.R. cooperation in space, which I have heard often, is in connection with Apollo–Soyuz, and it goes like this: "Apollo–Soyuz was supposed to affect Soviet behavior, yet it did nothing to prevent the Soviet military buildup in the 1970s, Soviet adventurism in Africa and the Middle East, Soviet crackdowns on dissidents. How, then, can we call it a success?" In fairness, that argument compares to the equally naïve expectation that Apollo–Soyuz would suddenly usher in a new era of peace and harmony. Critics and enthusiastic advocates both failed to recognize Apollo–Soyuz as a first small step toward building something completely new in space—the planting of a seed, a creative act. When the acorn didn't sprout into an oak tree at once and simultaneously multiply a thousandfold, we dug it up by the roots. The opportunities offered by the Space Age will never be realized by submitting it to the rules of the cold war it is meant to replace.

The warm, enduring relationship between commanders Tom Stafford and Alexei Leonov of Apollo–Soyuz transcends ideology.

162

It is the relationship of two heroic explorers who conquered the frontier of space together. Surely it is in democracy's interest to promote long-term policies of openness and cooperation that give the Staffords and Leonovs of this world a chance.

Of course, during this period of transition, policy-makers must take into account the vicissitudes of the cold war while exploiting the expansive opportunities of space. If, for instance, Soviet behavior reaches an extreme, cooperation will be called into question. But that should be a carefully reasoned, major policy decision, comparable to interrupting arms-control negotiations or breaking diplomatic relations. It should be considered with the full understanding that cooperation in space is of paramount long-term significance for the future of democratic values and institutions and that U.S. national interest benefits from its sustained pursuit.

The Soviets will no doubt attempt to exploit cooperation in every way they can—using it to seek concessions in other fields, to try to steal technology, to claim "parity" with the West, and so on. In response, rather than merely reacting to Soviet outrages in the usual predictable fashion, we should develop a new range of sustained cooperative policies. To discourage the Soviets from using cooperation to force concessions in other matters, joint missions should be designed so that our contribution is salvageable at any point. To reduce the risk of technology transfer, emphasis should be placed on coordinating separate missions, or, when necessary, designing "black box" instrument packages that might even self-destruct if tampered with. As it is, technology used for scientific missions in space has fewer secrets: the low-budget spacecraft that NASA's Solar System Exploration Committee has proposed for most scientific missions through the remainder of this century employs technologies already well known to the major spacefaring nations. As for our fear of Soviet propaganda claims of "parity," so long as space activities gradually grow more open and cooperative, using mechanisms that encourage free and open communication among the participants, there can be no parity. The

advantage will always reside with democracy. It's only when secrecy and oppressive control prevail that totalitarianism begins to
move toward parity. That's why it is so vital to keep space exploration moving toward openness and democracy.

The defeat of democratic openness in space would also be a
blow to deep, unfulfilled aspirations of the Soviet people. They
have never known democratic government, while we, to our good
fortune, have never known anything else. Even before the 1917
revolution that replaced an all-powerful tsar with an all-powerful
communist apparatus, the Russian people were living under a
suspicious and compulsively calculating authoritarian regime; they
still harbor deep feelings of inferiority toward the West, in part a
product of envy; and they suffer under an inefficient, stifling bureaucracy, as they have through most of their history. But that
same adversity has bred a people of extraordinary depth and di-
versity of feeling. We glimpse it in their literature and poetry,
which enjoys parity with that of any nation in the world. The
Russian people have known suffering almost unimaginable to us,
and they have survived and even triumphed in their way. The
Russians are a plodding people, compared to us, not given to sudden
changes of fashion, yet durable in ways we perhaps cannot understand. What is our best response to a courageous and enduring
people shackled as much by history as by ideology?

I would suggest a more clinical approach to U.S.–U.S.S.R. relations, using space as a primary, but not exclusive, opening wedge.
The differences between Russians and Americans are not genetic.
If we are patient (a common trait among Russians, comparatively
rare among Americans), if we develop policies that give sustained
encouragement to a gradual opening up of oppressive Soviet society, we will see slow but lasting results on behalf of ideals and
aspirations shared by all humanity.

None of the above implies a reduction of military strength, which
must be managed according to the strictest and most detached
assessment of Soviet capabilities, nor is it to suggest a policy of

youth festivals and world friendship meetings that Soviet propagandists love to exploit. But without letting down our defenses, and without indulging in fruitless love feasts, we can still encourage an expanded role for positive traits in the Russian personality, *provided we are consistent about it*. For enduring effect, we should pursue practical objectives, in space in particular, which will, at the points of contact, encourage a gradual evolution toward democratic openness, while, equally important, avoiding a slow evolution on our side toward secrecy and oppressive state control.

165

19 / SPACE WEAPONS

The debate over the Strategic Defense Initiative has produced an avalanche of verbiage, statistics, charts, and graphs intending to show whether or not the concept will work. Comparatively little attention has been paid to the larger question of the impact on American society of the longest and most massive top-secret high-tech project ever undertaken. What will be Star Wars' impact on scientific inquiry, economic productivity, democratic values and institutions, national and international priorities, the structure of the federal budget, other activities in space?

The space-weapons issue cries out for reexamination in that larger context. We already know that research on space-based and space-directed laser and particle beam weapons is underway in the U.S. and the U.S.S.R. We can argue over which country is doing more research today, but experience teaches that, no matter who's ahead, the other one will eventually catch up. It also has become clear that space-weapons systems, even if wholly successful, will only make one type of nuclear weapon obsolete (the ICBM) while inviting the Soviets to develop other nuclear systems the Strategic

Defense Initiative can't touch, such as nuclear terrorist devices. Nor will space weaponization halt with the deployment of the system currently envisioned. Star Wars will be followed by new generations of space weapons and counterweapons, including new weapons that will be capable of killing people by the thousands and millions.

A space-weapons researcher at the Lawrence Livermore National Laboratory in Berkeley, California, told *Newsweek* magazine (June 17, 1985): "The number of new space weapons designs is limited only by one's creativity." That kind of creativity doesn't belong in the vanguard of American policy for the Space Age, churning out new weapons "inevitabilities" that feed on themselves and may eventually consume us all.* Space-weapons researchers are now, in effect, writing United States policy extending far beyond their scientific objectives and their professional expertise, rendering the rest of us increasingly helpless to do anything but submit to their commands.

Perhaps it's time for the American people, including their political and military leaders, to regain control over America's destiny. Research on SDI may be necessary now, and those who pursue that research should be honored for meeting a national necessity. But that's all. Star Wars isn't the Holy Grail. It's a gruesome piece of machinery, incapable of mobilizing American ideals as a force for progressive change and bound to undermine American interests by making the tools of diplomacy hostage to a whole new array of wildly expensive weapons systems. The objective of American diplomacy should be to overcome the cold war that has responded to the Space Age with Star Wars. *That* is the real long-term problem posed by the Soviet Union.

The solution lies in the ability of Americans to take on exciting

---

* *As an indication of things to come, an Air Force Association weapons fair in Washington, D.C., in September 1985, included, among its dozens of defense industry exhibits, a presentation that showed SDI activities on one wall and SDI countermeasures on the opposite wall. Already, we are on the way to making Star Wars obsolete with new weapons. The process is endless.*

technical challenges and *make them into democratic experiences*. It's a matter of directional attitude. Although opposed to a space-weapons crash program, I deeply admire the willingness of its advocates to try to *do* new things; critics of SDI are often only negative. I'd just rather see America's positive can-do spirit applied to building a democratic space environment. How can we know it's impossible if we don't try? And if we don't try, who will?

20 / SPACE COOPERATION

The United States and the Soviet Union have contrasting concepts of negotiation. For us, negotiation means that parties settle their differences through a process of give-and-take. For the Soviets, negotiation is successful when one side (theirs) takes everything it can get and gives virtually nothing in return. One of their favorite tactics is to wait us out while promoting divisions on our side that create pressures for unilateral concessions. In the few instances when the Soviets have made concessions, they have often cheated on what they promised, and they give ground not when exposed but when their coldly calculated interests require it.

We know all that, or we should, but our own policy efforts break down when we fasten on it with voyeuristic rapture: "Look how awful they are! Look how they're trying to divide us! Look how they cheat!" It follows that they only understand brute force. So we must keep beefing up our brute force. They respond by beefing up their brute force, confirming our assumption and inviting more brute force in return. We might as well be apes. Meeting strength with strength, finding peace through strength, negotiating from strength, and other such primitive concepts, play a vital role in our relations with the Soviets, unfortunately; they should not be abandoned, but neither should they be enthroned as the only reality political leaders are capable of creating.

The real challenge is not to defeat the Soviets at their game, which we can't do without becoming more and more like them, and which brings out the worst on both sides, but to open new fronts in which the game is played by rules that advance American ideals and values in consonance with American interests, at home as well as abroad. Star Wars offers a starting point. It is clear that certain types of space-weapons research can't be monitored and therefore can't be considered during arms-control negotiations. But there will be a point, after all, when SDI activity will become visible, and both sides will reach it well before full deployment. Arms-control negotiators should seek to fix that point in the future, and make it a cutoff point. Whoever reaches it first will pause, and Congress will provide the funding necessary to insure that we get there first. We also will be prepared to move quickly beyond that point if necessary.

Having satisfied our real concern that the Soviets might beat us to Star Wars, we can initiate a new, broader, and more promising policy that emphasizes cooperative activity among spacefaring nations, according to democratic rules and procedures. Already the Soviets are actively courting the nations of Western Europe and Japan (witness the U.S.S.R.–Europe–Japan space fleet to Halley's comet). A broad U.S. space cooperation policy that engages the democracies of Europe and Japan could be used to guide the Soviets toward a regime in space such as they have never known on earth, under the flag of democracy. It would take years and decades. But at least we would be putting technology and democratic values to work in space, unitedly, on a course aimed at transcending the cold war.

21 / DOD AND NASA

The chief operations agency for manned cooperative missions designed by NASA and approved by the State Department ought to be the U.S. Air Force. The Air Force would carry out its cooperative activities under open-space rules. The transition shouldn't be difficult. The Apollo program, as we've seen, was directed by an Air Force general detailed to NASA along with scores of Air Force operations officers, and that open program was a resounding success.

Management of unmanned space science missions would be retained by NASA, but those missions would be administered in a broader context. In addition to performing basic research on a cosmic scale, civilian space scientists would serve as scouts for human exploration and settlement—designing and directing unmanned reconnaissance activities that pave the way for manned missions, and working with the Air Force in the design and operation of advance bases and laboratories on space stations and planets. Space science would be an activist, frontier profession, in every sense, as science in Antarctica is today and was on the American frontier in an earlier age.

Under that new arrangement, NASA would be a leaner, tougher, and more flexible agency, with greater responsibilities at two ends of the space policy spectrum. At one end, NASA would keep probing outward on the space frontier. At the other end, NASA would oversee rapid transfer of space technology to private enterprise so as to keep the United States competitive in a growing international space market.

Meanwhile, the Air Force would have recovered the traditional military role of managing large-scale expeditions of exploration, dating back in our country to the Lewis and Clark expedition at the turn of the eighteenth century. In accordance with that restored mission, the Air Force Academy and other Air Force institutions would become leaders in preparing new generations of commanders and support personnel for cooperative manned space missions. The Air Force might even establish a Stafford Training Institute as a counterpart to a Leonov Training Institute in the U.S.S.R., in honor of the two commanders of Apollo–Soyuz.

The mere suggestion that a military agency play a major role in space exploration, even under open-space rules, is bound to send tremors of anxiety through much of the civilian community. We must recognize that such anxiety is a relatively recent product of the cold war, which also polarized civilian-military perceptions and activities within our own country. Never in American history has the military mission been so self-consuming and so isolated from the nation at large. The situation virtually assures the perpetuation and escalation of cold-war confrontation. It is unhealthy and dangerous, and it must be corrected.

22 / NSA

Information obtained by the superb satellite surveillance resources of the NSA and related agencies should, whenever possible, be made public, in cooperation with other nations, with each step negotiated by the State Department. Findings that by inference reveal our maximum surveillance capabilities should remain secret. But that still leaves plenty of room for revealing information that could prove decisive in combating environmental problems which transcend national frontiers, such as air and water pollution and the natural causes of famine (drought, pest invasions, deforestation, etc.). In addition, information on troop movements worldwide collected by U.S. and U.S.S.R. surveillance satellites should be made public, gradually, in carefully negotiated stages. At first, such efforts would be opposed by nations who don't want their arch-rivals to know what they're doing (Iran and Iraq, India and Pakistan). But the competing superpowers can point to their own example, showing how mutually accepted satellite surveillance has been instrumental in avoiding military confrontation between the U.S. and the U.S.S.R. An incremental effort to open up and expand that practice might take advantage of such opportunities as policing a truce, when opposing sides would welcome third-party involvement. If it is developed with cautious persistence, as a *long-term* objective, a worldwide military surveillance program could eventually become a major force for avoiding conflicts between nations.

23 / SCIENCE

Over the years, as the quality of their work improved, Soviet space scientists increased their participation in international activities. Today they are exchanging information and ideas to a degree unimaginable a decade ago, and of a quality that more than holds its own. The members of this new generation of Soviet explorers are no doubt party loyalists or they couldn't hold their jobs; but they also have their eyes on a future without precedent in Soviet experience. From their position of expanding influence, they are beginning to explore new relationships that meet the unique challenges of the Space Age and that are inherently democratizing.

Of course, as Soviet space scientists become more international in their outlook and activities, it can be assumed that the KGB will try to exploit them for espionage. The KGB tries to exploit everything, cooperative or otherwise. But it is a terrible mistake to suggest, as some do, that the KGB is behind the entire process that is bringing Soviet space scientists into the international community—that, in effect, the Space Age is a KGB espionage plot. In reality, the Space Age is just the reverse—a powerful current for democratic openness. The KGB can't stop it. But the United States can, if we recoil from the democratic opportunities that space cooperation offers.

The internationally minded scientific community is a weapon for open democracy whose potential is unlimited in the Space Age. Out of necessity, as we have seen, the first wave of space explorers will be predominantly scientist-engineers united by shared objectives. Those who build the first base on the moon or Mars won't be knocking down trees with axes. They will be installing the most complex laboratories and life-support systems ever devised. Whatever their national or ideological backgrounds, all of them will be absorbed by common problems that have no counterpart on earth. If, over the next generation or two, all spacefaring nations are allowed to explore the space frontier together, the democratic current of the Space Age will grow into an overpowering tide.

24 / INDUSTRY

In the late eighteenth century, the industrial revolution permanently altered the character of society by replacing hand tools with power-driven machinery and concentrating manufacturing in large establishments called factories. During the nineteenth and early twentieth centuries, the forces unleashed by the industrial revolution were tamed as electricity, steam power, iron and steel production, assembly-line manufacturing, and the attendant reorganization of management and labor were perfected. In the late 1940s, there came a new high-technology revolution, led by the miniaturization of information technologies and their application to virtually every aspect of industry.

The advent of those new technologies coincided with the cold war and a U.S. military strategy based on maintaining technological superiority over the Soviets. As a consequence, a large proportion of the high-tech revolution's energy and imagination went into weapons production, leading to the development of a $100 billion a year peacetime defense industry, concentrated in aerospace manufacturing. "As a peacetime entity," wrote the president of the

Aerospace Industries Association, "it is a young industry, born in the wake of World War II to counter a Soviet threat and publicly supported, in the years since, only as long as and to the extent that such a threat was perceived." The coincidence of the cold war and the new high-tech revolution, with whole new industries associating their dynamism with the dynamism of the cold war which monopolized their activities, set in motion a process that would eventually threaten the efficiency if not the very character of American business activity on the frontier of economic development.

As noted earlier, the defense industry exhibits a number of traits that set it apart from other free-enterprise industries. They include monopoly or quasi-monopoly in the industrial sector, special and often secretive relationships in the government sector, protection from foreign competition, protection during lean years (to insure the defense industrial base), an overriding competition with the Soviets governed by rules that often undermine free-market efficiency and productivity.

Defense critics who argue that inefficiency can be corrected by greater competition among defense contractors miss a fundamental point. Many of the problems that bedevil the defense industry are traceable to the high-tech revolution itself. One key identifying characteristic of that revolution is the continuing refinement of ever more complex products, carried forward by new advances in information technology. Under the overriding national requirements of the cold war, those increasingly complex developments are channeled inexorably into defense.

Here is where it leads: Our new B-1 bomber will come with seven thousand maintenance manuals, totaling more than 1 million pages. Our new M-1 battle tank uses twice as much fuel (seven gallons per mile) and costs twice as much to repair as its predecessor. It comes with twenty-two repair and operations manuals, and is followed into battle by a lumbering support fleet of tow trucks, earth movers, and fuel trucks. Between 1980 and 1984, the number of aircraft in the U.S. arsenal increased by nine percent and the money spent on aircraft increased by ninety-one percent. "In the year 2054," says Norman Augustine, vice-president of Martin Marietta aerospace corporation, "the entire defense budget will go to purchase just one tactical aircraft. The aircraft will have to be shared by the Air Force and Navy three and a half days each per week, except for leap year, when it will be made available to the Marines for the extra day."

Augustine is dramatizing a process called structural disarmament. It begins to take effect when increased unit costs and reduced export markets lead to a downward slide in the number of weapons produced. The decline picks up speed as the weapons grow more complex and defense budgets reach their economic and political limits. Structural disarmament has become a major issue in Great Britain, where the number of ships and planes in the Royal Navy and the Royal Air Force are now half of what they were in the 1960s. The process has taken longer in the United States, thanks to the awesome generosity of American taxpayers, but we are finally moving along the downward slope, too. We'll really begin to feel its pull when the operating costs for dozens of new high-tech weapons systems and battle management systems, typified by the B-1 bomber and the M-1 tank, begin to take their toll on the federal budget—and that doesn't include SDI.

It is argued that structural disarmament can be avoided by shifting to less complex weapons systems. But I'm not sure that proposal will succeed in the present cold-war climate, either. If the Department of Defense moves away from the leading edge of high technology, passing the torch to civilian industry, the Soviets will find it all that much easier to steal technology for military purposes. Then they will have the advantage of *both* numbers and technology. On the other hand, if our defense policy continues to be guided by a strategy of technological superiority, the fruits of the high-tech revolution will be sucked into the defense sector more and more, until even the budgetary pressures of structural disarmament are overwhelmed by a new reality: sometime near the turn of the twenty-first century, the American people will be faced with only one alternative—the militarization of the American economy.

It is that as yet little-discussed alternative, which would fundamentally alter the character of our nation, which worries me most. I think it's the most likely outcome if we don't do something about the cold war itself—the East–West *relationship* that has produced this closed loop of insanity. The United States isn't Britain or France. We *must* maintain parity, at the minimum, with the Soviets. It is also true that the high-technology revolution will continue with or without the cold war. We thus risk finding ourselves, before too long, in a catch-22 situation: in order to protect ourselves from the Soviet threat at our front door, we will be forced to let totalitarianism in the back door. We will militarize our economy and undermine our democratic institutions in the name of democracy and national survival. I do not believe for a moment that the American military desire that outcome. They are trapped as we all are by a self-consuming process that current cold-war policies are not equipped to address.

But space offers a way out—perhaps the only way. We can't halt the cold-war high-tech production juggernaut, but we can redirect its purpose. If given a chance, space exploration and settlement can channel the intertwined high-tech revolution and U.S.–U.S.S.R. relationship into constructive activities that give the advantage to democratic practices in ways inconceivable when secretive confrontation prevails. Cooperation in space may be necessary, ultimately, to insure the triumph of democracy over repressive state control in the Space Age.

I know it's often alleged that a scaled-up space commitment, drawing on the same aerospace industry that produces weapons, will lead to the same problems of inefficiency and waste encountered in defense production. The argument is based on similarities in scale of major space and defense projects. But it ignores the *open* character of space exploration, which makes all the difference.

Professor Ezra Vogel of Harvard, author of the path-breaking book *Japan as Number One*, which first awakened Americans to the scope of Japan's economic challenge, has published a sequel, *Comeback*, which offers a response to Japan that will restore the initiative to the United States. At the top of his list of models for American-style success, Vogel places NASA's Apollo program. He describes how, during Apollo, NASA mobilized the scientific, engineering, and high-tech manufacturing resources of this nation in a manner that simply couldn't be employed for a major high-tech defense undertaking. Every step of the way, from design to production, Apollo was open to the most widespread public scrutiny. Participants benefited from open communication at all levels. The contribution of university research centers, so vital to the success of American high-tech enterprise, was sought without suffocating secrecy requirements and it was delivered with universal enthusiasm. To help ensure quality control, NASA easily recruited thousands of scientists, engineers, and managers from businesses and universities, and information flowed among them freely. Procurement was centralized and directed toward a clear target and fixed schedule—landing men on the moon in a decade. By contrast, defense procurement procedures are guided by competing military services coming up with duplicating requirements for an open-ended technological superiority that has no result other than its self-perpetuation. Apollo was going somewhere; it wasn't a preparedness exercise. Apollo was efficient in ways that are unavailable to the defense industry in the cold war, no matter how much we reform it.

Still, had Apollo been followed by a program of settlement on the moon, which would have extended it indefinitely, it might have suffered from certain efficiency problems also found in defense production. They can be traced to the monopolistic or quasi-monopolistic contracting required for large-scale high-tech activity. As with high-performance fighter-bombers and missiles, only a handful of companies could compete for lead contracts on projects on the scale of Apollo. The Apollo program avoided noncompetitive inefficiencies by being a relatively short-term, full-scale mobilization project that never really had a chance to develop the institutional inefficiencies which plague the defense industry. How can such long-term inefficiencies be avoided in space exploration?

Significantly, I think, the answer can be found by reversing a situation that contributed to Apollo's short-term success. Apollo was a national mobilization project. But now that the space industry has come of age in this country and abroad, an international long-term approach appears not only preferable but necessary. International cooperation would encourage greater *competition* for large-scale space activity by opening up a wide new range of joint-venture combinations for contractors, as the European Space Agency nations are already demonstrating. It's the best of both worlds: governments negotiate agreements in which a single nation takes the lead for one component of a project, acting through a company of that nation which may be working in alliance with companies of other nations. Defense industry simply can't operate with the same freedom and openness. *In space, cooperation encourages the efficiencies of open competition.*

Finally, expansive space exploration (not restrictive cold-war confrontation) is the appropriate environment for the high-technology revolution to realize its true potential. At every stage in human history, advances in technology are linked to the movement of peoples. The space shuttle can be traced backward in a direct line to the wheel. The rise and fall of civilizations, the depth and breadth of their contributions to human progress, is tied to their ability and willingness to move about and explore and to develop new tools for that purpose. Each advance is followed by a period of consolidation, but the quest always resumes. It's not a question of whether we must first solve all our social problems before breaking new ground. On the contrary, progress is a demonstrated function of movement. If our ancient forebears had remained around some Neolithic campfire, determined to cure all their social ills before striking out, we'd still be living in caves.

The diversion of the high-tech revolution to restrictive defense activity, rather than using it to initiate the next new expansive stage of human progress, is a historic aberration. That the most open and dynamic civilization in human history should be its helpless instrument is a tragedy and a waste. We need policies that allow American free enterprise to exploit the new frontier in space in ways that internationalize American ideals and bring about the truest fulfillment of America's destiny.

25 / PLANETARY EXPLORATION POLICY

The space shuttle and the space station are our principal manned space flight programs for the 1980s and 1990s, yet both suffer from the absence of a Space Age context for their activities.

The space shuttle was originally part of a manned Mars mission package conceived by Wernher von Braun in the 1950s which lost out to the Apollo moon program for political reasons. In 1969, the Mars package was presented to President Nixon, but only the shuttle emerged, forcing its operators to invent new justifications for their disconnected existence. They came up with satellite launching and various scientific experiments in zero gravity. It was as if Columbus had justified his discovery fleet as a means of testing certain scientific concepts in a floating environment. His chances would have dropped to zero. Our space planners have been more successful, but not by all that much. Shuttle and space station have gone through one tortuous justification after another, as we keep backing into the Space Age with our eyes fixed firmly on the ground.

Shuttle designers were forced to take another giant step away from reality in the 1970s when Congress showed signs that it wouldn't even approve President Nixon's rootless proposal. In order to win Congress over, NASA made the impossible claim that the shuttle would eventually pay for itself.* But, outside the context of the interplanetary objectives for which it was originally conceived, there was no way the shuttle could justify itself, much less pay for itself. Already, it is becoming apparent that the only agency that can "afford" the shuttle, in its distorted operational context, is the Department of Defense and its Star Wars program, where the bottom line is an incidental principle. Early in 1985, NASA signed a contract making DOD its primary customer and chief lobbyist for congressional funding, which will only distort the shuttle's mission even more.

Something similar appears likely to occur for the second component of the Mars mission package, scheduled for construction in 1993—the space station. Right now, the $8 billion space station is being justified as a scientific laboratory and a manufacturing center for materials produced more efficiently in space. But Space Industries, Inc., of Houston, has already announced plans to launch a smaller version of our space station, at less than one-tenth its cost, four years sooner, in 1989. No doubt, the official 1993 version will be more elaborate. Still, by the time our $8 billion space station is constructed in 1993, it will be in serious danger of going the way of the shuttle, and looking to DOD more and more to justify its existence. It will serve primarily as a weapons-testing platform, with its laboratory and commercial activities consigned to more cost-effective free-flying laboratories and manufacturing centers comparable to the one being launched by the Houston firm. The labs and manufacturing centers will rotate around the weapons platform and be supplied by it—a perfect symbol of the sort of Space Age society we are backing into.

---

* *After NASA was forced to fantasize a mission for the shuttle, shuttle development began to show inefficiencies suggestive of a cold-war weapons program.*

185

But if we restore the interplanetary exploration target for which shuttle and space station were conceived, and assign appropriate lead times for each stage toward its attainment, the entire picture changes. Shuttle and space station would then be properly recognized as infrastructure meant to support space exploration, development, and settlement. As such, the justification for investment in them compares to the justifications for federal investment in the roads and railroads that opened the American continent, or the interstate highway system that still depends on federal funds for its existence.

In that Space Age operating context, so-called space commercialization will realize its true potential. When the early focus is on commercialization at the expense of exploration, we pull up short and start looking for pay-offs almost before we've left the ground. Instead, as the first modest commercial possibilities are being tested, let the exploration keep moving outward. Discoveries we can't now imagine are the ones that will offer the greatest commercial returns.

The chief differences between the Space Age and previous ages of civilization are in the unprecedented size, scope, and lead times of its Space Age activities, a global perspective of the targets (the moon in its entirety, Mars, asteroids, giant orbiting structures), and a globalistic approach to the task that organizes the human and material resources of our planet for a coordinated advance into the cosmos. Our human species will rise to the challenge, and begin to reap its benefits, when perceptions and policies are adjusted to accept those differences. Only then will we experience the full potential of the Space Age as a force for constructive change.

The period of transition from the cold war to the Space Age will begin with renewed space cooperation between the U.S. and the U.S.S.R. in a broad international framework, governed by goals and procedures that point beyond the cold war toward democratic space. We can initiate that transition today by mobilizing worldwide support for an International Space Year in 1992, highlighted by a number of coordinated manned and unmanned missions. In preparation for the International Space Year, beside stepped-up scientific exchanges and planning, U.S. and Soviet negotiators might resume where they left off in 1978 and arrange a series of complementary shuttle–Salyut missions, joined by the European Space-lab. They would be followed, in 1992, by the construction of U.S. and U.S.S.R. space stations with communications and docking compatibilities and with participation from other nations. The space stations would be designed to serve as launch platforms for coordinated missions deeper into space and for assembling materials for large orbiting industrial facilities. At some point near the turn of the century—sooner or later, depending on the international climate—manned rocket ships would leave space-station launchpads on a coordinated mission to Mars. They would set up a permanent base. Supply ships with fresh crews would follow. As the years passed, the men and women of the Mars project would report exciting new discoveries. Perhaps one of their discoveries, springing from a seed that an earlier generation dared to plant, would be a triumphant awareness of their common humanity.

APPENDIXES

I THE SPACE COOPERATION RESOLUTIONS

Between 1982 and 1985, I introduced seven congressional resolutions dealing with international cooperation in space, the texts of which are reprinted here.* The resolutions follow a progression that reflects a continuing effort to capture the distinctive character of the Space Age. The first in the series, introduced in 1982, warns against a space arms race, describes the potential of space cooperation, and calls for an international space station. The second resolution, introduced in 1983, calls for renewal of the U.S.–U.S.S.R. space cooperation agreement, although the space-station proposal remains in the background. The third resolution, introduced in 1984, is nearly identical to its 1983 predecessor. After negotiations in the Senate and the House over its language, the 1984 resolution passed both houses of Congress and was signed into law by President Reagan. Evidence of the 1982 origins of that public law survive in its "whereas" clauses. The Mars and International Space Year resolutions, which conclude the series, are more oriented toward encouraging specific Space Age activities on their own merits; that is, they reach beyond the cold war.

* Technically, nine resolutions were introduced, but two of them (relating to Mars exploration and an International Space Year) were reintroductions of resolutions offered in the same session of Congress, with modest changes. For those two, only the final versions are included here.

Congressional resolutions come in three categories, each of which is represented here:

1. A *Senate Resolution* takes effect if passed by a majority vote in the Senate. (Each of these categories has an identical version in the House.)

2. A *Senate Concurrent Resolution* takes effect only if passed by both the Senate and the House (hence the term "concurrent"), giving it a bit more bite than a Senate Resolution. Senate and Senate Concurrent Resolutions are called "nonbinding" because they lack the force of law.

3. A *Senate Joint Resolution* takes effect if it is passed by both houses of Congress *and* signed by the President. If the President signs a Senate Joint Resolution, it becomes a "binding" public law that the executive branch of government must implement. If the President vetoes it, the measure dies, unless Congress overrides his veto by a two-thirds majority in both the Senate and the House.

Whether binding or not, and whether it passes or not, a congressional resolution can be an influential instrument of government. Members of Congress publicly debate it. The executive branch of government is required to deliver written comments on it. Congressional committees may hold hearings on it which arouse national interest. The discussion a pending resolution provokes inside and outside government often leads to important policy changes.

Resolutions are written in dense legal language and follow a tightly restricted format. In all cases, they consist of a series of "whereas" clauses which summarize the issue, followed by a series of "resolved" clauses which prescribe a course of action. It is a challenge to any legislator who cares about language to breathe some life into the "whereas" clauses and structure the "resolved" clauses to allow flexibility in administering the activity proposed in the resolution without subverting its intent.

With one exception, the resolutions reproduced hereafter are discussed in the text of this book. The exception, Senate Concurrent Resolution 137, is meant to call the attention of the White House and the State Department to an often overlooked problem faced by federal agencies which are ordered to implement bilateral agreements signed at summit conferences: the U.S. signers of the agreements neglect to provide the affected federal agencies (NASA, Department of Agriculture, HUD, etc.) with the funds necessary to do the job.

APPENDIXES

September 29, 1982

Whereas the United States and the Soviet Union are on a course leading toward an arms race in space which is in the interest of no one;

Whereas the United States and the Soviet Union will drift into an arms race in space as prisoners of events unless preventive measures are taken while a choice still exists;

Whereas an arms race in space would open the door to a range of weapons systems whose introduction would further destabilize an already delicate military balance, perhaps permanently foreclosing hope for successful arms control agreements, requiring immense open-ended defense expenditures unprecedented in scope even for these times;

Whereas the prospect of an arms race in space between the United States and the Soviet Union has aroused worldwide concern expressed publicly by the governments of many countries, including most of the allies of the United States, such as Australia, Canada, France, the Federal Republic of Germany, India, Japan, and the United Kingdom of Great Britain;

Whereas the first decisive step in an arms race in space would involve the use of orbiting space stations for testing weapons, which would proceed inevitably from the tensions and suspicions generated by competing American and Soviet space stations;

Whereas the 1972–75 Apollo–Soyuz project involving the United States and the Soviet Union and culminating with a joint docking in space was the most successful cooperative activity undertaken by those two countries in a generation, thus proving the practicability of a joint space effort;

Whereas the opportunities offered by space for prodigious achievements in virtually every field of human endeavor, leading ultimately to the colonization of space in the cause of advancing human civilization, would probably be lost irretrievably were space to be made into yet another East–West battleground; and

Whereas allowing space to become an arena of conflict without first exerting every effort to make it into an arena of cooperation would

193

amount to an abdication of governmental responsibility that would never be forgotten: Now, therefore, be it

Resolved, that it is the sense of the Senate that the President should—

(1) initiate talks with the Government of the Soviet Union, and with other interested governments of countries having a space capability, with a view toward exploring the possibilities for a weapons-free international space station as an alternative to competing armed space stations; and

(2) submit to the Congress, at the earliest possible date, but not later than June 1, 1983, a report detailing the steps taken in carrying out paragraph (1).

SEC. 2. The Secretary of the Senate shall transmit a copy of this resolution to the President.

SENATE CONCURRENT RESOLUTION 16—
RELATING TO COOPERATIVE EAST–WEST VENTURES IN SPACE

March 10, 1983

Whereas the United States and the Soviet Union are on a course leading toward an arms race in space which is in the interest of no one;

Whereas the prospect of an arms race in space between the United States and the Soviet Union has aroused worldwide concern expressed publicly by the governments of many countries, including most of the allies of the United States, such as Australia, Canada, France, the Federal Republic of Germany, India, Japan, and the United Kingdom of Great Britain;

Whereas an arms race in space would open the door to a range of new weapons systems that would seriously threaten global stability, undermine the prospects for successful arms control agreements, and create pressures for new defense expenditures unprecedented in scope even for these times;

Whereas the 1972–75 Apollo–Soyuz project involving the United States and the Soviet Union and culminating with a joint docking in space was a significant success, thus proving the practicability of a joint space effort;

Whereas, shortly after the completion of the Apollo–Soyuz project, and intended as a follow-on to it, the United States and the Soviet Union signed a formal agreement to examine the feasibility of a Shuttle–Salyut

Program and an International Space Platform Program, but that initiative was allowed to lapse;

Whereas the United States signed a five-year space cooperation agreement with the Soviet Union in 1972, renewed it in 1977, then chose not to renew it in 1982, despite numerous scientific benefits accruing to the United States as a result of joint activities initiated under that agreement;

Whereas the opportunities offered by space for prodigious achievements in virtually every field of human endeavor, leading ultimately to the colonization of space in the cause of advancing human civilization, would probably be lost irretrievably were space to be made into yet another East–West battleground; and

Whereas allowing space to become an arena of conflict without first exerting every effort to make it into an arena of cooperation would amount to an abdication of governmental responsibility that would never be forgotten: Now, therefore, be it

Resolved, that it is the sense of the Congress that the President should—

(1) renew the 1972–1977 agreement between the United States and the Soviet Union on space cooperation for peaceful purposes;

(2) initiate talks with the Government of the Soviet Union, and with other governments interested in space activities, to explore the opportunities for cooperative East–West ventures in space as an alternative to an arms race in space, including such ventures as joint space medicine and space biology activities; joint missions to the Moon, Venus, Mars, Jupiter and Saturn; other activities in the field of planetary science; manned space exploration; a weapons-free international space station; and

(3) submit to the Congress at the earliest possible date, but not later than December 1, 1983, a report detailing the steps taken in carrying out paragraphs (1) and (2).

SENATE JOINT RESOLUTION 236—

EAST–WEST COOPERATION IN SPACE

AS AN ALTERNATIVE TO A SPACE ARMS RACE

February 9, 1983

Whereas the United States and the Soviet Union are on a course leading toward an arms race in space which is in the interest of no one;

Whereas the prospect of an arms race in space between the United States and the Soviet Union has aroused worldwide concern expressed publicly by the governments of many countries, including most of the allies of the United States, such as Australia, Canada, France, the Federal Republic of Germany, India, Japan, and the United Kingdom of Great Britain;

Whereas an arms race in space would open the door to a range of new weapons systems that would seriously threaten global stability, undermine the prospects for successful arms control agreements, and create pressures for new defense expenditures unprecedented in scope even for these times;

Whereas the 1972–75 Apollo–Soyuz project involving the United States and the Soviet Union and culminating with a joint docking in space was a significant success, thus proving the practicability of a joint space effort;

Whereas shortly after the completion of the Apollo–Soyut project, and intended as a follow-up to it, the United States and the Soviet Union signed a formal agreement to examine the feasibility of a Shuttle–Salyut Program and an International Space Platform Program, but that initiative was allowed to lapse;

Whereas the United States signed a five-year space cooperation agreement with the Soviet Union in 1972, renewed it in 1977, then chose not to renew it in 1982, despite numerous scientific benefits accruing to the United States as a result of joint activities initiated under that agreement;

Whereas the opportunities offered by space for prodigious achievements in virtually every field of human endeavor, leading ultimately to the colonization of space in the cause of advancing human civilization, would probably be lost irretrievably were space to be made into yet another East–West battleground; and

Whereas allowing space to become an arena of conflict without first exerting every effort to make it into an arena of cooperation would amount to an abdication of governmental responsibility that would never be forgotten: Now, therefore, be it

Resolved, by the Senate and House of Representatives of the United States of America in Congress assembled, that the President should—

(1) renew the 1972–1977 agreement between the United States and the Soviet Union on space cooperation for peaceful purposes;

196

(2) initiate talks with the Government of the Soviet Union, and with other governments interested in space activities, to explore the opportunities for cooperative East–West ventures in space as an alternative to an arms race in space, including cooperative ventures in such areas as space medicine and space biology, space rescue, planetary science, manned and unmanned space exploration; and

(3) submit to the Congress at the earliest possible date, but not later than October 1, 1984, a report detailing the steps taken in carrying out paragraphs (1) and (2).

SENATE JOINT RESOLUTION 236
(AS AMENDED BY CONGRESS)—RELATING TO
COOPERATIVE EAST–WEST VENTURES IN SPACE

Signed into law by President Reagan on October 30, 1984
(Public Law 98-562)

Whereas the United States and the Soviet Union could soon find themselves in an arms race in space, which is in the interest of no one;

Whereas the prospect of an arms race in space between the United States and the Soviet Union has aroused worldwide concern expressed publicly by the governments of many countries;

Whereas the 1972–75 Apollo–Soyuz project involving the United States and the Soviet Union and culminating with a joint docking in space was successful, thus proving the practicability of a joint space effort;

Whereas, shortly after the completion of the Apollo–Soyuz project, and intended as a follow-up to it, the United States and the Soviet Union signed an agreement to examine the feasibility of a Shuttle–Salyut Program and an International Space Platform Program, but that initiative was allowed to lapse;

Whereas the United States signed a five-year space cooperation agreement with the Soviet Union in 1972, renewed it in 1977, then chose not to renew it in 1982;

Whereas the United States recently proposed to the Soviet Union that the two nations conduct a joint simulated space rescue mission;

Whereas the Soviet Union has not yet responded to the substance of this proposal; and

Whereas the opportunities offered by space for prodigious achievements in virtually every field of human endeavor, leading ultimately to the colonization of space in the cause of advancing human civilization, would probably be lost irretrievably were space to be made into yet another East–West battleground: Now, therefore, be it

Resolved, by the Senate and House of Representatives of the United States of America in Congress assembled, that the President should—

(1) endeavor, at the earliest practicable date, to renew the 1972–77 agreement between the United States and the Soviet Union on space cooperation for peaceful purposes;

(2) continue energetically to gain Soviet agreement to the recent United States proposal for a joint simulated space rescue mission; and

(3) seek to initiate talks with the Government of the Soviet Union, and with other governments interested in space activities, to explore further opportunities for cooperative East–West ventures in space, including cooperative ventures in such areas as space medicine and space biology, planetary science, manned and unmanned space exploration.

SENATE CONCURRENT RESOLUTION 129—
RELATING TO SPACE RESCUE

June 28, 1984

Whereas the Treaty of Principles Governing the Activities of States in the Exploration and Use of Outer Space, Including the Moon and Other Celestial Bodies promotes international cooperation and understanding;

Whereas the Treaty on Principles Governing the Activities of States in the Exploration and Use of Outer Space, Including the Moon and Other Celestial Bodies states that astronauts should be regarded as envoys of mankind in outer space and all possible assistance shall be rendered to them in outer space and on celestial bodies by astronauts of other States Parties to the Treaty;

Whereas the Agreement on the Rescue of Astronauts, the Return of Astronauts and the Return of Objects Launched into Outer Space calls upon contracting parties in a position to do so, if necessary, to extend assistance in search and rescue operations to personnel of a spacecraft who have suffered accident or are experiencing conditions of distress;

Whereas the United States, Canada, France, and the Soviet Union are currently in a highly successful satellite-aided search and rescue program (COSPAS / SARSAT) involving coordinating the activities of United States, Canadian, French and Soviet Union equipment and satellites; Now, therefore, be it

Resolved, that it is the sense of the Congress that the President should—

(1) seek understandings and / or agreements with other nations to plan for space station activities that would permit space rescue operations and other emergency assistance in space;

(2) seek understandings and / or agreements with other nations for exchange of scientific and technical information that would aid in such space rescue operations and other emergency assistance pursuant to the Agreement on the Rescue of Astronauts, the Return of Astronauts and the Return of Objects Launched into Outer Space;

(3) examine other opportunities for mutually beneficial international coordination of U.S. permanent space station programs.

SENATE CONCURRENT RESOLUTION 137—RELATING
TO CERTAIN SCIENTIFIC EXCHANGE AGREEMENTS
BETWEEN THE UNITED STATES AND THE SOVIET UNION

September 5, 1984

Whereas since 1958, agreements between the United States and the Soviet Union have sponsored exchanges in the fields of science and technology, education, culture, and information, but activity under those agreements has declined in recent years;

Whereas on June 27, 1984, President Reagan announced plans to revive many of the bilateral agreements, stating that "certainly nothing is more worthy of our attention than finding ways to reach out and establish better communication with the people and the government of the Soviet Union";

Whereas on June 27, 1984, the President specifically mentioned agreements in the fields of environmental protection, housing, health, agriculture and oceanography, which are among a number of science and technology agreements negotiated between the United States and the Soviet Union;

Whereas, even under the best circumstances, United States participation in science and technology activities with the Soviet Union has been limited by an absence of funds specifically earmarked for activities under those agreements, such as travel funds and funds for arranging conferences and exchanging scientific papers; and

Whereas unless adequate funding is provided, the objectives sought by the President in his June 27, 1984, announcement may not be effectively realized: Now, therefore, be it

Resolved, by the Senate (the House of Representatives concurring), that it is the sense of the Congress that adequate funding should be provided to carry out existing bilateral scientific exchange agreements between the United States and the Union of Soviet Socialist Republics.

SENATE JOINT RESOLUTION 46—RELATING TO
NASA AND COOPERATIVE MARS EXPLORATION

February 7, 1985

Whereas President Reagan has called upon NASA to develop concrete goals beyond the space station that "will carry us well into the next century";

Whereas the original objective of United States space planners in the 1950s was the planet Mars, but it was replaced by a lunar mission for political reasons;

Whereas in 1969, members of a presidential task force again recommended a manned Mars mission as a logical follow-up to the successful Apollo program, with that mission to be launched from a space station, but it was rejected for budgetary reasons;

Whereas a manned Mars mission is within the reach of existing technology and could be carried out at an estimated one-half of the cost of the Apollo program in constant dollars;

Whereas the U.S.S.R. has made known that Mars is the objective of its manned space program;

Whereas recent Soviet successes in long duration space flight and Soviet development of a heavy-lift launch vehicle that far exceeds United States capabilities have been accompanied by authoritative reports that the Soviets are actively preparing for a manned Mars mission, for perhaps as early as the 1990s;

Whereas a U.S.–U.S.S.R. race to Mars would involve massive wasteful expenditures and redundancies that would be contrary to the best interest of all parties concerned;

Whereas Mars exploration is of immense scientific and social significance but without significance in terms of space weapons development;

Whereas the United States and the U.S.S.R. have scheduled unmanned scientific missions to Mars for this decade, but those missions have not yet been coordinated to insure maximum scientific return;

Whereas on October 30, 1984, the President signed a resolution passed unanimously by both Houses of Congress calling for renewal of the U.S.–U.S.S.R. space cooperation agreement that was allowed to lapse in 1982: Now therefore, be it

Resolved, by the Senate and House of Representatives of the United States of America in Congress assembled, that it is the sense of the Congress that the President, as part of his committed effort to renegotiate the U.S.–U.S.S.R. space cooperation agreement, should direct the Administrator of NASA, in consultation with the Secretary of State, to—

(1) explore the opportunities for cooperation on an already-scheduled Soviet mission to the Mars moon Phobos in 1988 and an already-scheduled United States Mars Geochemical / Climatology Orbiter mission in 1990, to insure maximum scientific return from both missions;

(2) prepare a report, in association with nongovernmental space scientists, examining the opportunities for joint East–West Mars-related activities, including an unmanned Mars sample return and all activities that might contribute to an international manned mission to Mars;

(3) submit to the Congress at the earliest practicable date, but no later than October 1, 1985, a report detailing the steps taken in carrying out paragraphs (1) and (2).

SENATE JOINT RESOLUTION 177—
RELATING TO AN INTERNATIONAL SPACE YEAR

July 17, 1985

Whereas the year 1992 is the 500th anniversary of the discovery of America by Christopher Columbus;

Whereas Spain will commemorate the discovery of America by launching an Hispanic satellite in 1992;

Whereas 1992 is the 75th anniversary of the Russian revolution and space-related commemorative events are reportedly planned by the Soviet Union;

Whereas 1992 is the 35th anniversary of the International Geophysical Year, hereinafter referred to as IGY, when the first artificial satellites were launched, thus marking the beginning of the space age;

Whereas an International Geosphere / Biosphere Program is planned for the early 1990s as a sequel to the IGY, but its space activities will be limited to earth observation;

Whereas space exploration has made enormous strides since the IGY and deserves concerted worldwide commemorative recognition and engagement as well;

Whereas 1992 appears to be ideally suited for such recognition and engagement: Now, therefore, be it

Resolved, by the Senate and House of Representatives of the United States of America in Congress assembled, that it is the sense of the Congress that the President should—

(1) endorse the concept of an International Space Year, hereinafter referred to as ISY, for 1992, perhaps extending into 1995;

(2) consider the possibility of discussing an ISY with other foreign leaders;

(3) direct the Administrator of NASA, in association with representatives of the State Department, the National Academy of Sciences, the National Science Foundation, and other relevant public and private agencies, to initiate interagency and international discussions that explore the opportunities for an ISY in the 1992–1995 time frame, including possible missions of international character and related research and educational activities;

(4) submit to the Congress at the earliest practicable date, but no later than March 15, 1986, a report detailing the steps taken in carrying out paragraphs (1), (2), and (3), including descriptions of possible international missions and related research and educational activities.

1986 NASA AUTHORIZATION CONFERENCE REPORT:
INTERNATIONAL SPACE YEAR PROVISIONS

It is the sense of the conferees that the year 1992 is ideally suited to the establishment of an International Space Year (ISY). The year 1992 marks the five hundredth anniversary of the discovery of America by Christopher Columbus. Spain will commemorate the discovery of America by launching a Hispanic communications satellite in 1992. Moreover, 1992 is the thirty-fifth anniversary of the International Geophysical Year (IGY), when the first artificial satellites were launched, thus marking the beginning of the space age. As a sequel to the IGY, an International Geosphere/Biosphere program is planned for the early 1990s, but its space activities will be limited to Earth observation. The conferees believe that space exploration has made enormous strides since the IGY and deserves concerted worldwide commemorative recognition and engagement. In addition to providing commemorative attention, the conferees believe that an International Space Year in 1992 could help maximize budgetary efficiency and scientific gain.

It is the sense of the conferees that the President should endorse the concept of an International Space Year for 1992 and consider the possibility of discussing the ISY with other foreign leaders. In addition, the Administrator of NASA, in association with other relevant public and private agencies, should initiate interagency and international discussions that explore the opportunities for an ISY in 1992. Such discussions should address possible missions and research and educational activities of an international character, including the possible inclusion of current plans and programs into an ISY framework.

The conferees have agreed on the language contained in section 115 in the conference report that requires the President to submit to Congress at the earliest practicable date, but not later than May 1, 1986, a report on any action taken with respect to the establishment in 1992 of an International Space Year. The report shall include descriptions of possible international missions and related research and educational activities and such other activities as the President may deem appropriate.

II U.S.–U.S.S.R.
SPACE COOPERATION AGREEMENT

In May 1977, the United States and the Soviet Union renewed a five-year space cooperation agreement. When the agreement came up for renewal again in 1982, the United States pulled out. The text of the 1977 agreement follows.

AGREEMENT BETWEEN THE UNITED STATES OF AMERICA
AND THE UNION OF SOVIET SOCIALIST REPUBLICS
CONCERNING COOPERATION IN THE EXPLORATION
AND USE OF OUTER SPACE FOR PEACEFUL PURPOSES

The United States of America and the Union of Soviet Socialist Republics;

Considering the role which the U.S.A. and the U.S.S.R. play in the exploration and use of outer space for peaceful purposes;

Striving for a further expansion of cooperation between the U.S.A. and the U.S.S.R. in the exploration and use of outer space for peaceful purposes;

Noting the positive cooperation which the parties have already experienced in this area;

Desiring to make the results of scientific research gained from the exploration and use of outer space for peaceful purposes available for the benefits of the peoples of the two countries and of all people of the world;

Taking into consideration the provisions of the Treaty on Principles Governing the Activities of States in the Exploration and Use of Outer Space, including the Moon and Other Celestial Bodies, as well as the Agreement on the Rescue of Astronauts, the Return of Astronauts, and the Return of Objects Launched into Outer Space;

Encouraged by the progress made in the course of mutually agreed activities pursued under the Agreement Between the United States of America and the Union of Soviet Socialist Republics Concerning Cooperation in the Exploration and Use of Outer Space for Peaceful Purposes, signed May 24, 1972;

In accordance with the General Agreement between the United States of America and the Union of Soviet Socialist Republics on Contacts, Exchanges and Cooperation in Scientific, Technical, Educational, Cultural, and Other Fields, signed June 19, 1973, and in order to develop further the principles of mutually beneficial cooperation between the two countries;

Have agreed as follows:

ARTICLE 1

The Parties will continue to develop cooperation in such fields of space science and applications as space meteorology; study of the natural environment; exploration of near earth space, the moon and the planets; space biology and medicine; satellite search and rescue systems; and, in particular, will cooperate to take all appropriate measures to encourage and achieve the fulfillment of the Summary of Results of Discussion on Space Cooperation Between the U.S. National Aeronautics and Space Administration and the Academy of Sciences of the U.S.S.R., dated January 21, 1971, periodically renewed.

ARTICLE 2

The Parties will carry out such cooperation through their appropriate national agencies by means of mutual exchanges of scientific information and delegations, and meetings of scientists and specialists of both countries, and also in such other ways as may be mutually agreed. Joint Working Groups may be created for the development and implementation of appropriate programs of cooperation.

ARTICLE 3

The Parties will take all necessary measures for the further development of cooperation in the area of manned space flight for scientific and practical objectives, including the use in joint flights of compatible docking and rendezvous systems derived from those developed during the experimental flight of Apollo and Soyuz spacecraft in July 1975. Joint work in this direction will be carried out in accordance with the Agreement Between the U.S. National Aeronautics and Space Administration and the Academy of Sciences of the U.S.S.R. on Cooperation in the Area of Manned Space Flight, dated May 11, 1977.

ARTICLE 4

The Parties will encourage international efforts to resolve problems of international law in the exploration and use of outer space for peaceful purposes with the aim of strengthening the legal order in space and further developing international space law and will cooperate in this field.

ARTICLE 5

The Parties may by mutual agreement determine other areas of cooperation in the exploration and use of outer space for peaceful purposes.

ARTICLE 6

This agreement shall enter into force May 24, 1977 and shall remain in force for five years. It may be modified or extended by mutual agreement of the Parties.

Done at Geneva this 18th day of May 1977 in duplicate in the English and Russian languages both equally authentic.

III U.S.–U.S.S.R. MANNED SPACE-FLIGHT AGREEMENT

Also in May 1977, NASA and the Soviet Academy of Sciences signed an interagency agreement calling for cooperation in manned space flight. Then, in 1978, after scientists from the two countries had begun discussions, the United States pulled out. The text of the manned space-flight agreement follows.

AGREEMENT BETWEEN THE U.S.S.R. ACADEMY OF SCIENCES
AND THE NATIONAL AERONAUTICS AND SPACE ADMINISTRATION OF THE U.S.A.
ON COOPERATION IN THE AREA OF MANNED SPACE FLIGHT

In accordance with the Agreement on Cooperation in the Exploration and Use of Outer Space for Peaceful Purposes between the U.S.S.R. and the U.S.A., dated May 24, 1972, and taking into account the results of discussions held in Washington, October 12–19, 1976, between the delegation of the U.S.S.R. Academy of Sciences, headed by the Chairman of the Intercosmos Council of the U.S.S.R. Academy of Sciences, Academician B. N. Petrov, and the delegation of the National Aeronautics and Space Administration of the U.S.A., headed by the NASA Deputy Administrator, Dr. A. M. Lovelace, the Academy of Sciences and NASA agree to undertake the following steps for further development of co-operation between the U.S.S.R. and U.S.A. in the exploration and use of outer space for peaceful purposes.

I. *Study of the Objectives, Feasibility and Means of Accomplishing Joint Experimental Flights of a Long-Duration Station of the Salyut-Type and a Reusable "Shuttle" Spacecraft (Salyut–Shuttle Program)*

In view of the fact that the long orbital stay-time of the Salyut-type station and the capabilities of the shuttle spacecraft commend their use for joint scientific and applied experiments and for further development of means for rendezvous and docking of spacecraft and stations of both nations, the two sides agree to establish two Joint Working Groups (JWGs) of specialists, charging them with studying the objectives, feasibility and means of carrying out a joint experimental program using the Soyuz / Salyut and Shuttle spacecraft:

—a JWG for basic and applied scientific experiments.

—a JWG for Operations.

Within 30 days after the Agreement becomes effective, the sides will inform each other of the initial leaders and composition cf these JWGs. The work of both Joint Working Groups should begin simultaneously. The composition of the JWGs can be changed or enlarged at any time as necessary. Appropriate sub-groups can be formed.

In their studies, the JWGs should proceed on the assumption that the first flight would occur in 1981. The final date would be set in the course of the joint work.

First Phase of the Joint Working Groups' Activity

The following preliminary project documents should be prepared within 6–12 months after the agreement comes into effect:

—preliminary proposals for scientific experiments;

—preliminary technical proposals for carrying out the program;

—preliminary schedules for implementing the program.

Second Phase of the Joint Working Groups' Activity

The JWGs should prepare the following definitive documents within one year of joint work in the second phase:

—a technical description of the joint program and its realization;

—a scientific program for the joint flight;

—a schedule for conducting the joint work;

—an organizational basis for implementing the program;

—a list of additional joint technical documentation which may be required.

The sides will make the final decision on implementing the program at the end of the second phase of the JWGs' activity.

The working period of the JWGs in the first and second phases of their activities can be shortened.

Each side will consider the accommodation on its spacecraft of payloads proposed by the other side for flight in the Shuttle–Salyut program. Such accommodation will be undertaken where both sides agree that the payloads concerned are of mutual value and interest.

II. *Consideration of the Feasibility of Developing an International Space Platform in the Future (International Space Platform Program)*

Both sides recognize that no commitments are made at this stage concerning the realization of any project for creating an international space platform.

The sides agree to establish a Joint Working Group of specialists for preliminary consideration of the feasibility of developing an International Space Platform on a bilateral or multilateral basis in the future.

The JWG will carry out its work on the basis of studies conducted by each side independently and also by the two sides jointly, proceeding from each of the following stages to the next as may be mutually agreed;

—define at the first stage the scientific and technical objectives which would warrant the use of such a space platform.

—consider possible configurations appropriate to the objectives identified.

—formulate proposals on the feasibility and character of further joint work which may be desirable in this field.

At the first stage of its activity, the group will work in close coordination and contact with the JWGs set up to consider ways to realize the Salyut–Shuttle program.

The sides will appoint the initial leaders and members of the JWG for this program within two months after the agreement goes into effect. This JWG should formulate preliminary proposals on possible scientific-technical objectives which could be achieved by an international station one year after beginning its work.

BIBLIOGRAPHY

During the preparation of articles, speeches, and congressional resolutions on space cooperation, I often consulted the Congressional Research Service. CRS, as it is known, is a division of the Library of Congress, which was established to provide congressional committees and individual members of Congress with background information at their request. I wish there was some way to cite all those anonymous CRS researchers who have assisted my legislative activities concerning space and related issues, but at least they deserve acknowledgment alongside sources cited below, including a few printed CRS reports available for public distribution. (Complementary to CRS is the Office of Technology Assessment, an arm of the Congress specializing in large-scale studies of complex technical issues, examples of which are cited below.) I am also grateful to the organizers of the 1984 "Case for Mars" conference, and particularly Tom Meyer, for sending me a selection of their proceedings in advance of publication, to supplement the published report of their 1981 meeting. The following selected list includes titles that I found especially useful not only for information but also, in some instances, for the reflections they provoked.

Aviation Week & Space Technology, weekly aerospace publication, McGraw-Hill. Basic weekly reading.

Berkner, Lloyd V. "Secrecy and Scientific Progress," *Science,* May 4, 1956.

Boone, W. Fred. *NASA Office of Defense Affairs: The First Five Years.* NASA, 1970.

Boston, Penelope P. et al. *The Case for Mars.* American Astronautical Society, 1984.

Bradbury, Ray et al. *Mars and the Mind of Man.* Harper & Row, 1973.

Chalk, Rosemary. "Commentary on the NAS Report," in *Science, Technology, and Human Values,* Winter 1983.

Chapman, Margaret, and Marcy, Carl, eds. *Common Sense in U.S.–Soviet Trade.* American Committee on East–West Accord, 1983.

Clarke, Arthur C. *1984: Spring—A Choice of Futures.* Del Rey, 1984.

Committee on Foreign Relations, United States Senate. "East–West Cooperation in Outer Space." A hearing report. U.S. Government Printing Office, 1984.

David, Leonard. "Blueprint for a Red Planet." Paper presented at the 1984 meeting of the International Astronautical Federation, in Lausanne, Switzerland.

De Vigny, Alfred. *The Military Necessity.* Humphrey Hare, London, 1953. Translation of a work originally published in 1830.

Ezell, Edward C. "Man on Mars: The Mission That NASA Did Not Fly." Paper presented at the annual meeting of the American Association for the Advancement of Science, in Houston, Texas.

———, and Ezell, Linda. *The Partnership: A History of the Apollo–Soyuz Test Project.* NASA, 1978.

Friedman, Louis D., and Sagan, Carl. *US/USSR Cooperation in Exploring the Solar System.* A Planetary Society special report, 1985.

Goetzman, William H. *Army Exploration in the American West, 1803–1863.* University of Nebraska Press, 1979.

Hampton, H. Duane. *How the U.S. Cavalry Saved Our National Parks.* Indiana University Press, 1971.

Joint Economic Committee, Congress of the United States. "East–West Technology Transfer: A Congressional Dialog with the Reagan Administration." U.S. Government Printing Office, 1984.

Logsdon, John. *The Decision to Go to the Moon.* MIT, 1970.

———. "The Policy Process and Large-Scale Space Effort," in Space Humanization Series, 1979.

———. "The Space Shuttle Decision: Technology and Political Choice," *Journal of Contemporary Business,* Winter 1979.

Lubin, Nancy et al. *U.S.–Soviet Cooperation in Space.* U.S. Government Printing Office, 1985. OTA technical memorandum.

Luxenberg, Barbara A. et al. *World-Wide Space Activities.* U.S. Government Printing Office, 1977. CRS study.

McDougall, Walter A. *The Heavens and the Earth: A Political History of the Space Age.* Basic Books, 1985.

Michener, James. *Space.* Random House, 1982.

Morrison, David, and Hinners, Noel W. "A Program for Planetary Exploration," *Science,* May 6, 1983.

National Aeronautics and Space Administration. *Outlook for Space.* U.S. Government Printing Office, 1976.

Oberg, James E. *Mission to Mars.* Meridian, 1983.

———. *The New Race for Space.* Stackpole, 1984.

———. *Red Star in Orbit.* Random House, 1981.

Rogers, Thomas F., Chandler, Philip P. et al. *Salyut: Soviet Steps Toward Permanent Human Presence in Space.* U.S. Government Printing Office, 1983. OTA technical memorandum.

Sagan, Carl. *Broca's Brain.* Ballantine, 1979.

———. *Cosmos.* Random House, 1980.

Sheldon, Charles II et al. *Soviet Space Programs, 1976–1980.* U.S. Government Printing Office, 1981. CRS study.

———. *Soviet Space Programs, 1971–1975.* U.S. Government Printing Office, 1976. CRS study.

———. *Soviet Space Programs, 1966–1970.* U.S. Government Printing Office, 1971. CRS study.

Smith, Marcia S. *Mars: The Next Destination for Manned Space Flight?* U.S. Government Printing Office, 1984. CRS report.

——— et al. *United States Civilian Space Programs, 1958–1978.* U.S. Government Printing Office, 1979. CRS study.

Snow, Charles Percy. *Science and Government.* Harvard University Press, 1961.

Space Science Department, Science Applications International Corporation. "Manned Lunar, Asteroid, and Mars Mission." A study for the Planetary Society, 1984.

Sullivan, Walter. *Assault on the Unknown.* McGraw-Hill, 1961.

Thomas, Lewis. "Scientific Frontiers and National Frontiers: A Look Ahead," *Foreign Affairs,* Spring 1984.

Turner, Stansfield. *Secrecy and Democracy: The CIA in Transition.* Houghton Mifflin, 1985.

Vogel, Ezra F. *Comeback.* Simon and Schuster, 1985.

von Braun, Wernher. *The Mars Project.* University of Illinois Press, 1953.

———, and Ley, Willy. *The Exploration of Mars.* Viking, 1956.

Washburn, Mark. *Mars at Last!* Abacus, 1979.

Wasserburg, Gerald J. et al. *Strategy for Exploration of the Inner Planets.* National Research Council, National Academy of Sciences, 1978.

Williamson, Ray et al. *International Cooperation and Competition in Civilian Space Activities.* U.S. Government Printing Office, 1985. OTA study.